BUY THIS BOOK!

Understanding Advertising And Getting The Most Out Of Your Advertising Dollar

BUY THIS BOOK!

Understanding Advertising And Getting The Most Out Of Your Advertising Dollar

by Raj Marwah

Cartoons by Bruce Baldwin

American Marketing Association

Copyright © 1991 by Raj Marwah
Published by the American Marketing Association
Chicago, Illinois.

First published in 1989 by Post Publishing Company Limited, Bangkok, Thailand.

Cover Design by Raj Marwah, Kanit Nontapaoraya, and Frank Leone
Cartoons by Bruce Baldwin

Library of Congress Cataloging-in-Publication Data

Marwah, Raj, 1947-
    Buy this book! : understanding advertising and getting the most
out of your advertising dollar / by Raj Marwah ; cartoons by Bruce
Baldwin.
    p.   cm.
    ISBN 0-87757-215-1 :
    1. Advertising. 2. Marketing. I. Title.
HF5823.M334 1991
659.1—dc20
                                                                    91-10793
                                                                    CIP

Printed in the United States of America

Dedicated to my wife,
Eveline,
who left the land
of her birth
— like me —
to join up for a
bigger adventure.

Contents

Pick any of these easy-to-digest chapters and get a quick insight into the subject that interests you.

Introduction.

"Minds are like parachutes. They only function when they are open."

Sir James Dewar

THANK you for buying this book.

It is a collection of articles about advertising that I wrote two years ago for syndication in a couple of major newspapers soon after I came back to Asia. After almost two decades away.

I came back full of enthusiasm and a burning need to create great advertising. I came back from places as diverse as New York, London, Brussels, Geneva, Dusseldorf and Sydney to the continent that gave me birth.

I quickly discovered that advertising in Asia had the same joys and disappointments as other parts of the world. Because people share the same hopes, fears, need, aspirations and dreams all over the globe.

I found myself making the same impassioned speeches in defence of my work as I would anywhere else. Passionate, because when we don't sell our product - the advertising we create - to our clients who are going to pay for it, it dies.

It suffers the worst fate an endeavour can meet in our business: *it does not appear in any medium.* I decided to accept the invitation to write in the business pages of regional newspapers a series on advertising that would help lay some common ground and help me sell my work to clients. It was a successful series of articles.

Now, as a collection of those articles goes to the presses in the form of a book, democracy has made great strides all over the world. And as democracy breaks out, people are beginning to demand their right to choose a product, service or idea as well as their right to vote.

Markets as well as minds are opening up around the globe.

I hope this book will help you *win* in any market, irrespective of whether it is sophisticated or still developing. Because this book, by nature of its subject - advertising - deals with people. And people, in essence, do not change their basic drives whatever system they thrive, or labour, under.

"It took millions of years for man's instincts to develop," said the great adman Bill Bernbach, *"and it will take millions more for them to vary. It is fashionable to talk about changing man. A communicator must be concerned with unchanging man, with his obsessive drive to service, to be admired, to succeed, to love, to take care of his own."*

Out in Forsayth, Queensland, among the ruins of the old goldfields in an area that really defines the harshness of the Australian outback with its "appalling extremes of flood or drought," Peter Cole-Adams writing for The International Herald Tribune came back with this charming headline from an old goldfield undertaker's advertisement: "WHY LIVE

AND BE MISERABLE WHEN YOU CAN BE DECENTLY BURIED BY DINNY O'DWYER FOR SIX POUND TEN?"

Australia definitely shaped my views about *directness* in communication as I wrestled with quotes from legends like Reggie Ansett, who founded Ansett Airlines, and had a great answer for many of the so-called marketing experts who sat down to confound him with documents and science: "I have a simple marketing theory," he is supposed to have said. "When you cater to the masses, you will dine with the classes. And when you cater to the classes, you will dine with the masses!"

There you have it. Mass marketing, simply explained.

I don't know if I can hope to do better than this.

I hope this book helps you become a better communicator.

When I started out in the business, I found that books were all I had to help me find my way. People were either too busy, or were unwilling to trust me till I had some experience. And, as every beginner knows, it is difficult to get experience till somebody trusts you with the job.

Like the Cuban astronaut who came back after a successful mission on a Russian spaceship. Fidel Castro goes to see him at Havana airport. The nation's TV has been playing nothing but this man's life for the last three days. All of Cuba is watching, breath bated. The charismatic leader reaches out to shake the Cuban astronaut's hands after kissing him on both cheeks, and notices that they are both bandaged and bloody and wants to know what happened up in space to damage the airman's hands? "What can I tell you?" says the poor astronaut, "Senor Castro, the Russian astronauts and I got along fine up there. Except when I tried to do something myself. Then they would slap my hands and say 'don't touch this and don't touch that'!"

The suggestions made in this book are fairly basic, and basics are precisely what many so-called experts (who will patronisingly obstruct you) tend to overlook.

I saw a funny movie last year where the bumbling hero tries to take a photograph of some people in a remote land. On hearing their cries of protest he retreats quickly, and turns to the headman patronisingly to say "I see! I understand! They are shouting at me to tell me in their language that if I take their photograph, they are worried that the camera will steal their soul, yes?"

"No," says the headman, "they are trying to tell you that you neglected to take the lens-cap off!"

This book, like that village headman, also offers you those two bits of advice - take off the lens-cap before you shoot and don't underestimate your target audience.

May I suggest that you read it the way it was written: one chapter a week.
I wish you good shooting.

Raj Marwah,
March 1991,
Huka Lodge, New Zealand.

I
The real resource is people.

HELLO, I'M JENKINS.
HEAD OF ACCOUNT SERVICE

"Weapons are an important factor in war, but not the decisive one; it is the man and not the materials that counts."

- *Mao Tse-Tung*

SOMEONE once said that advertising is a lot like cannibalism: they are both a people business.

Obviously, this someone was never in the advertising business — or any business for that matter. Because, as anyone in business will tell you, people are crucial to all enterprises. Even the totally automated factory needs someone to push the button. Or to decide *when* to push the button.

It needs people.

In advertising, it so happens that people, and the knowledge and expertise they contain in their brains — between their ears — are all that you are really paying for when you decide to advertise. So what they recommend you do with each dollar they spend on your behalf makes their level of know-how exceptionally important.

"My entire inventory," a famous Madison Avenue ad agency supremo once said "goes down the elevator at 5.30 p.m. every night." This agency chief had worked out what his real assets were: the copywriters, the art directors, the visualizers and paste-up artists, the account directors and executives, the media planners and buyers, the research heads, the finance people. Without them, he had no product to sell.

People.

In advertising, people — and how you choose them, motivate them and, most important, listen to them — can make your ad budget work twice as hard, or just make a ripple instead of a splash in the marketplace.

Let's face it, though advertising is almost as old as the first tribe where the first Neanderthal brandished the biggest club, as a science, it is less than 70 years old. Modern advertising dates back to the time when Claude Hopkins wrote a book called "Scientific Advertising" and forever changed the way its practitioners go about this business in this century.

"I know that half of every dollar I spend on advertising is wasted," a well known manufacturer of consumer goods, Lord Leverhulme, once said, *"but the problem is I don't know which half!"*

In the few decades since this remark was made, advertising has leaped through unimaginable breakthroughs that enable experts to pretty much tell you "which half" as well as how to minimize wastage and to give you the optimum benefit from your budget in almost every area. This ancient reservoir of ignorance about our business has forced advertising practitioners to also become marketing experts — which is probably a good thing.

But still, today, we have advertisers in some parts of the world who treat their ad budget like 'games time' and advertising itself as a totally hit-or-miss affair. When the times are good (and sales are up), they will often say it was their R&D people who thought up or re-formulated their product or congratulate their distribution network or sales staff or even some one-off incentive that worked well at the point of sale.

But when times get tough, they often expect their ad people to take the blame.

This is quite amazing when you think of how you deal with your lawyer or your doctor. The clarity with which you share your problems, the bond of trust which you create and the faith and dedication with which you listen to and follow their advice can make a monumental difference to your legal or physical health.

And yet, when it comes to advertising (the public face that we put on your product or service), advertisers often tell ad agencies *what* to say in their ads, *how* to say it and *which* medium to use and *when!*

Advertisers who understand how advertising works make fortunes from its correct use. In the following chapters, Understanding Advertising will help you expand your knowledge of the business of advertising. And that, in turn, could help you make — or increase — your fortune.

II

How to recognize a great ad.

"When you want to do battle, muster all your forces, not neglecting any of them, a battalion sometimes decides a battle."

- Arthur Wellesley, Duke of Wellington

know what you're thinking: "I don't need to know how to recognise a good ad — its greatness will be evident the second I see it!"

Well, that's a bit like saying that you know the face you see every morning in the mirror is going to be beautiful. Because an ad *you* think is great is simply reflecting your taste and your opinion of your business.

Important though this line of thinking might be to you, this particular criterion is utterly worthless from the point of view of the consumer. Remember, please, that the person whom you are aiming at — the consumer who will hear or see or read your ad — is as human as you are. He (or she) is much more interested in what *they* think is good for *them.*

Nobody knows your business as well as you do. By that same token, an ad agency is much more likely to know *their* business better than you: how to craft a commercial communication that persuades people to buy a product or service or idea.

However, since not all ads that we see or hear these days can be called good (never mind great!), I will give you seven questions you could ask yourself to help you spot a hard-working ad before you spend a single dollar.

Frank Lowe, chairman of Lowe-Howard Spinks in London and a man who has *commissioned* some of the best advertising in the world in his career as an agency chief, once told me: *"Advertising is a business that everybody approaches with their mouth open: from the chairman's wife to the tea-lady. Everyone, unfortunately, has a point of view on advertising that you and I might labor hard to create, in any country."* If you are new to the business of advertising or marketing, a few rules that you read here could help you keep your mouth shut and, instead, your eyes and ears open. The improved advertising that can result will amaze you.

1. - *Will it get noticed immediately (by people other than just your family, friends, relatives and employees)?*

Without any hesitation, this is the first criterion you should apply when presented with an ad for approval. Remember, for example, that people buy a newspaper for the news; they listen to radio, perhaps, for the music; they turn on television to be entertained.

Harsh though it is, reality taught us long ago that nobody dips into a medium for its commercial content. So, the onus is on the advertisement to grab the reader's or viewer's attention. And the ad must do this amid a veritable clamor of other ads shouting for attention in the marketplace of the medium. Not to mention the programs or news headlines that constantly seduce your target's attention.

2. - *Is your ad going to get noticed? Instantly?* If it isn't noticed, it won't be read. And if it isn't read, it's dead. It's a waste of money.

3. - *Is it interesting?*

Ed McCabe, the recently retired advertising genius who created Scali, McCabe and Sloves in New York, once said to me: *"Only 10% of advertising created anywhere is any good at all."*

While this is a harsh judgment, the fact remains that most advertising can be so boring that it can put people to sleep. And nobody buys much while they are asleep.

4. - *Is the advertising too safe?*

Safe advertising is probably the most dangerous advertising of all.

'Safe' advertising can be created, for example, when the advertiser sees a great and successful campaign for a competitive product and tells his agency: "Give me a series of ads like those great ads for Brand X."

This means that you are simply spending your own precious ad dollar to help remind the consumer about your competitor's product! Remember, the competitor got to their hearts and minds before you did. And unless you have a bank account deeper than the South China Sea, you won't win many of them with your 'similar' story.

'Safe' advertising is also created when product managers and marketing managers decide not to take any 'risks' for fear of upsetting their bosses.

This sort of advertising is bland and boring and dies unseen and unheard in the marketplace.

'Safe' advertising is risky because it carries the disadvantage of never being noticed by consumers who are exposed to literally hundreds of advertising messages.

In the history of commerce, nobody ever made a dollar without being brave. Why should your approach to the advertising of your product be any different to your approach to the rest of your business?

If you really want to be safe, be original. You'll increase your chances of being effective proportionately.

5. - *Is the ad relevant?*

It's easy to grab attention in an ad if you drape a semi-clothed lady on the bonnet of a car — if what you're selling is lingerie.

If you're trying to sell the car, you are in trouble. Most people won't remember the car, let alone the marque.

The rule about relevancy sounds obvious when you read it, but look around. Advertising is full of ads that have nothing to do with the product they are selling.

24

6. - *Is the message telegraphic?*

Look at the headline of this chapter.

The series is called "Understanding Advertising". The title says: "How to recognize a great ad."

This means that the author is aiming single-mindedly at people like you who are interested in increasing their knowledge of advertising. And if you didn't feel a need to learn more ways to recognize a great ad, you would have given up reading this long ago.

The consumer is busy and preoccupied with a thousand concerns other than whatever we are trying to sell. We have to more than grab the attention of our target audience. We have to do it quickly!

David Ogilvy used to say that very few people ever really notice an ad, let alone read past the headline.

In any medium today, as the pace of life gets faster, speed in getting the message across is even more important than ever before.

Read the headlines in this morning's newspaper. Communicating information quickly is such an art that newspapers employ special people to do the job. They are called sub-editors.

And in a newspaper, your ad has to compete with their craft. But they have more interesting material to work with. It is difficult for a mere ad to compete quickly with stories of murder, rape, a landing on Mars or a civil war!

7. - *Is your ad single-minded?*

You might think of 10 good things you want to say about your product or service. Unfortunately, if the ad is good enough to fulfil the six criteria above and be seen and read and noticed, the consumer will still 'take away' only one idea from the ad. If you're lucky.

So try not to ask too much from your agency. Let research, discussion, your sixth sense, agency opinion — anything — help you and your people agree on *one* idea. Then let your advertising hammer it home.

The rule of thumb is: one ad, one idea.

One benefit. One promise. Brilliantly executed. Look again at any of the great ads you loved *and remembered* last year and you'll know that they employed this philosophy.

Conclusion:

Obviously, this chapter cannot and should not cover the more obvious requirements of an advertising practitioner's craft.

We have to take for granted that your ad agency knows what it is doing: that the right market has been identified; the correct tone of voice is being used; the ad is persuasive and helps the consumer change his/her mind or see your product in a new light; the ad is crafted so that it addresses one person instead of the world at large; each ad is a one-to-one communication — a newspaper might reach thousands, but one person reads it at one time!); the media chosen are the best for reaching the audience you want and their use is innovative and impactful.

But asking the seven questions before you approve the ad will help your advertising agencies do a better job for you.

It will set them free and help them fly.

III

A few thoughts from a master of the game.

WANTED.
Tea lady with
in depth knowledge
of Bill Bernbach's
advertising
philosophy.
To work in
marketing dept.
of major company.
Phone 2677881
for appointment.

"Nobody counts the number of ads you run; they just remember the impression you make."

- Bill Bernbach

PEOPLE with a nodding acquaintance with advertising often come across the sayings of David Ogilvy, a giant of his time.

But people who are familiar with the works of the late Bill Bernbach (the original Volkswagen ads, the famous Polaroid campaign, the "We try harder because we are No. 2" campaign for Avis) know that he was a genius who advanced the science of advertising by a few million light years.

He is a first among equals who helped fashion advertising as we know it today: Mr. Young and Mr. Rubicam and Mr. Rosser Reeves and Mr. Leo Burnett.

Bill Bernbach is dead.

But he left behind some thoughts and philosophies that sparkle with life in these quotations you are about to read. In these words, his spirit is very much alive.

Every one of these lines can help you when you try to brief your ad agency.

Each of these thoughts can stand by your side as you try to evaluate the impact of your advertising budget tomorrow.

Here is Bill Bernbach, speaking for himself:

"Just because your ad looks good is no insurance that it will get looked at. How many people do you know who are impeccably groomed but dull?"

"We are so busy measuring public opinion that we forget that we mould it. We are so busy listening to statistics that we forget we can create them."

"Today's smartest advertising style is tomorrow's con."

"Be provocative. But be sure your provocativeness stems from your product. You are not right if in your ad, you stand a man on his head just to get attention. You ARE right if you have him on his head to show how your product keeps things from falling out of his pockets."

29

"I wouldn't hesitate for a second to choose the plain-looking ad that is alive and vital and meaningful, over the ad that is beautiful but dumb."

"Our job is to sell our clients' merchandise, not ourselves. Our job is to kill the cleverness that makes us shine instead of the product. Our job is to simplify, to pluck out the weeds that are smothering the product's message."

"Rules are what the artist breaks, the memorable never emerged from a formula."

"You can say the right thing about a product and nobody will listen. You've got to say it in such a way that people will feel it in their gut. Because if they don't feel it, nothing will happen."

"Properly practiced creativity MUST result in greater sales more economically achieved. Properly practiced creativity can lift your claims out of the swamp of smotherness and make them accepted, believed, persuasive, urgent."

"If your advertising goes unnoticed, everything else is academic."

"It's not just what you say that stirs people, it's the way you say it."

"Nobody counts the number of ads you run; they just remember the impression you make."

"You can get attention, and really make people resent you, if you do it with an unrelated gimmick. They won't like you for that."

"You can have everybody coming in on time, everybody leaving on time, all work finished on the due day, and still have a lousy ad, and fail."

"I can put down on a page a picture of a man crying, and it's just a picture of a man crying. Or I can put him down in such a way as to make you want to cry. The difference is artistry — the intangible thing that business distrusts."

"To keep your ads fresh, you've got to keep yourself fresh. Live in the current idiom and you will create in it. If you follow and enjoy and are excited by the new trails in art, in writing, in industry, personal relationship ... whatever you do will naturally be of today."

"It took millions of years for man's instincts to develop, it will take millions more for them to even vary. It is fashionable to talk about changing man. A communicator must be concerned with unchanging man, with his obsessing drive to service, to be admired, to succeed, to love, to take care of his own."

"In communications, familiarity breeds apathy."

"It is ironic that the very thing that is most suspect by business, that intangible thing called artistry, turns out to be the most practical tool available for it. For it is only an original talent that can vie with all the shocking news events and violence in the world for the attention of the consumer."

"All of us who professionally use the mass media are the shapers of society. We can vulgarize that society. We can brutalize it. Or we can help lift it onto a higher level. 99

I have nothing more to add to this chapter.

Rather than reading any comments I might have, I urge you to read each Bernbach line again till you know it by heart.

I do.

And these quotations, all this *practical* wisdom, coming from one man — one brain — fills me with awe and respect.

This is knowledge that can make you money.

IV

How to get a job in advertising.

WHEN I GROW UP
I WANT TO BE A
CORPORATE ACCOUNT
STRATEGY PLANNER.

"I offer neither pay nor quarters nor provisions, I offer hunger, thirst, forced marches, battles and death. Let him who loves his country in his heart, and not his lips only, follow me."

- Guiseppe Garibaldi

MUST you? I mean, have you seriously considered much less taxing occupations like that of biochemist or astronaut? Or more predictable fields like medicine or law? Stand-up comics certainly have more fun, modelling agents suffer less rejection and some sausage factory assembly line workers gain more glory than many advertising people.

Is it because you think you are just right for the job?

After 16 years of interviewing people around the world, I have found that candidates who think they are natural whizz kids are in fact most often destined to fail, often miserably. It is the miniscule minority who don't think they know everything and are desperately trying to learn, who stand a chance of making it in this business.

And if all you want to do is learn, it is perhaps best to point out that advertising is a business like any other. It is demanding, compelling, frustrating, time-consuming, often nerve-wracking and, if you put in the right mixture of blood, sweat and tears, sometimes exhilarating. You won't find too many people in our business who are willing to give up precious time to teach you, like at college.

Well, if you haven't given up (and are still reading this chapter), what kind of an advertising job do you want?

Don't read this chapter any further if you want to immediately become an account executive or a media buyer, or a financial controller (yes, we have those in advertising!), a researcher or account planner.

I have spent most of my career in advertising as a creative director and hence I do not feel qualified to tell you, in any depth, how to become any one of those other experts.

Read on only if you wish to join a creative department (that's the one with the people who actually try to create the ads).

Now that we have established that you want to become a writer or art director, there's one more thing to keep in mind: these two roles are not terribly different.

An art director, for instance, needs good ads in his porfolio just like a writer. And pictures that go with the ads just need to be roughs, like those in a writer's folio. Pictures make ideas easier to understand, but roughs need to be exactly that: quick and simple, rough and ready. Remember, you are not being hired for your ability to draw (the ad agency has artists for this purpose); you are being hired for your ability to *think*. Beautiful drawings are not evidence of your ability to think.

In advertising, people who draw earn a lot less than people who think.

And if the previous paragraph has given you the feeling that you are actually going to need a folio of ads, you're right.

Dave Trott, creative partner of Gold, Greenless Trott, one of the hottest ad agencies in London, is one of the best spotters of undiscovered talent in the world. My conversations with him revealed the following points to remember when getting your folio together for an interview, and some of these are my own observations, in no particular order:

1. We are not interested in all you have done. We are interested in the *best* you have done. So a few good ads beat quantity every time.

2. We are more interested in your ability to think: creatively, innovatively, logically. We are interested in your ability to communicate: telegraphically, dramatically, memorably. We are not interested in your personality. If you think you have a great personality, go join a theater group. And anyway, most creative directors will first ask you to leave your folio before they see you. Which means your scintillating personality will not count for much. You might be sitting on a beach in Pattaya or Tahiti while your work is being evaluated.

3. Don't come in if you are afraid of rejection. If you want pats on the back (and to be told how clever you are), stay in school. And if you think your work is so fantastic, you'll need to be there when you sell (you can't - see point#2, above). If you think you are more intelligent than the people who are criticizing your work, stay at home. Advertising is a communication business, and if one person, just one person, does not understand what you're saying in your ads in a certain target group, you have failed.

4. Meet with some people you respect to learn about what is good and bad work before you set up your interviews. And don't use this opportunity (which is meant for picking their brains) to con them into hiring you. If you do that, they will smile politely, and next time you call, they will not be available.

5. Always tell the truth, always use logic and always be willing to learn. In this, advertising is like any other business.

6. If you are going to create ads specially for the interview because you have not worked in advertising before, choose campaigns instead of single ads, because that's what we do most often in the real advertising world. This means you need to generate a campaign idea, a unity of thought that, perhaps, becomes a strapline or positioning platform for the campaign.

7. Forget about puns and alliterative pyrotechnics. In your advertising, try to demonstrate your ability to use logic in a selling argument. The best and simplest way is

I found that this ad, a version of which I have written in other markets, gave me the best response from exactly the kind of people I was hunting.

37

to create ads that make people think: "This ad is selling me a product that is better than the one I am about to buy." This way, you are not wasting an advertising budget selling people things they don't want to buy. You are talking to someone who is already interested, and helping him lean towards your product. An obvious (and the obvious is often the best) way is to try to put your product next to competition. Avoid, at this stage, certain products like colas, soap powders, chocolate bars and so on which are often more or less the same. Look for a Unique Selling Proposition (USP) that makes your product better. Is it bigger? Smaller? Can it save a life? Is it safer than its competitors? Do you get more of it? Does it last longer? Then use the principles of advertising to make a campaign for the product. However, this sort of approach may need careful handling in those countries where comparative advertising is discouraged. But it does give the person evaluating your work a better idea of your ability to isolate a USP and to communicate it effectively.

Well, we seem to have run out of space, so I will end by giving you some names of books that might help you learn some of the principles of advertising before you go job-hunting in the creative arenas of advertising:

Scientific Advertising by Claude Hopkins; *Confessions of an Advertising Man* by David Ogilvy; *Making Ads Pay* by John Caples; and, for the fun of it, *From the People Who Gave You Pearl Harbor,* by Jerry Della Femina. Plus anything you can find written by Rosser Reeves. I also usually recommend *The Art of War* by Sun Tzu because it has everything - and nothing - to do with advertising.

Some of these books are between 10 and 40 years old, but you have to learn the rules before you break them.

Best of luck.

V

Positioning a product in the marketplace (Part 1).

AND THIS IS WHERE WE PLAN TO POSITION YOUR PRODUCT.

"Go, Sir, gallop, and don't forget that the world was made in six days. You can ask me for anything you like, except time."

- *Napoleon Bonaparte*

IF the first humans that a Martian met after landing in any peace-loving, thriving part of this planet were to be marketing or advertising people, he'd be on the blower to his space station quite smartly with the message: "Hold everything, there is a WAR going on here!"

I mean, look at the language that we use.

We don't just create ads, we create *campaigns*. Instead of introducing new products, we *launch* them (like a Minuteman from a secret silo). The initial ads are called a *flight* (like arrows from a corporate quiver); a cluster of ads is called a *blitz* (which would do Rommel proud); cheaper brands are called *fighting* brands created solely to attack the competition and the brand is *killed* if it doesn't perform. We *probe* for new positions: devise *strategies* to gain the high ground and *defend* our product with all our *might*.

The Twentieth Century Adman (many of whose ilk now, incidentally, dress in a mode that is not totally dissimilar to Martian haute couture) would then explain to the Space Traveller that the war, really, was being fought using the marketplace for a battle ground and it was all about making a better product and a lot of money.

"All you have to do," our Adman would explain, "is to build a better mousetrap and the world will beat a path to your door. Create Unique Selling Propositions! Create an image and then flog the hell out of it! We've got marketing techniques, coupons, money-off discounts, point-of-purchase displays, deals for shelf space, box-top promotions and advertising schemes with heavy media weight and books on how to get great ads."

The funny thing about the above scenario is: the Martian is right and the Adman is wrong.

Because, yes, there is a war going on down here.

And no, the battleground is not the marketplace or your R&D department or factory.

The killing field where the product lives or dies, where it really becomes a leader or an also-ran, is the consumer's mind.

Because what the Adman did not tell the Martian was why seven out of 10 new products introduced by so-called marketing management expert companies in the last 50 years *died* in the marketplace around the world.

There is no such thing as a sure thing.

Here are these companies with all the weaponry, all the discount deals and shelf

41

An Australian approach to positioning for an underwear ad.

space — the introductions, distribution and initial acceptance in the trade — that you could expect in an ideal-case scenario in those books they teach in business colleges. And they fail.

Think of it. A seven out of 10 failure rate. If commercial failure were a crime, wasting billions of dollars would surely require capital punishment. And yet everyday we see the same mistake again and again and again.

How is it that it is almost impossible to dislodge a brand leader? Why do line extensions of one brand almost always lead to a weakening of its original market share (in the mother brand)? How does a brand often live or die on the strength or weakness of its name alone? Why is it more important for an advertiser to first look for a hole in the consumer's mind before he can even hope to gain a niche in the marketplace? And if he finds this hole to position his product, how can he reposition the competition by using its own strength against itself?

Positioning

It is so important a subject that I will devote the next two chapters to this discussion.

But if you don't have the patience to wait that long, I urge you to read a very good book (a book that is used in quite a few business colleges — but, sadly, to little effect!) called "Positioning: The Battle For Your Mind".

A couple of guys in New York called Al Ries and Jack Trout wrote three articles on April 24, May 1 and May 8, 1972, in *Advertising Age,* the trade magazine for advertising in America, and started a controversy that, in some markets, still threatens a brand's life and, in some cases, professional careers.

This was later expanded to form a book that has proved itself quite a few times over in this last decade.

To define positioning in the marketing context, you start by throwing away any ideas you have about "product positioning." Positioning is not something you do to the product (or service, or idea, or yourself, or whatever it is that you are trying to sell), but it has everything to do with the place it ends up occupying in the prospect's mind. This means any change you make to the product in price, or name, or packaging is relevant only in terms of what *positioning* you can help it gain in the prospect's mind.

And getting the right position can take money.

In 1987, for instance, Procter & Gamble spent one billion and 435 million and 454 thousand dollars in America alone, on advertising, just to protect the position it has gained for its products!

The above figure, of course, includes advertising-related expenditures like direct marketing, co-ops, POPs, promotions and coupons, etc, but it is still a healthy wad of cash to put on the poker table they call The Ultimate Marketplace: the U.S. of A.

Read about positioning if you don't have that kind of money to throw around. It can help you increase market share by learning from the mistakes of others.

Because the next person who talks to you about positioning might not be a Martian.

It could be a competitor as he overtakes you, laughing all the way to *his* bank.

VI

Positioning a product in the marketplace (Part 2).

LOOK MABEL!
STRATEGICALLY DARING
POSITIONING, CONSIDERING
THE CATEGORY, OF COURSE.

"God is always with the strongest battalion."

- *Frederick The Great*

I N my career in advertising, I have been lucky enough to work for, or lead, the creative departments of advertising agencies that handle advertising for brand leaders.

Heading up a creative department in such an advertising agency gives one a marvellous overview of what makes brands into leaders.

And keeps them up there.

For instance, the first thing you discover (very much a vindication of the Ries and Trout book mentioned in the last chapter) is that once you are a leader, you are pretty much unassailable.

This means that 'leader brands' develop an inexorable momentum simply by virtue of their leadership position in the first place!

That's amazing when you say it, but obvious when you think of it.

I am not giving away any secrets when I tell you that, in many cases, these leaders were simply brands that came in first.

First. Not first in the market, but first in the consumer's mind.

And in that statement is the heart of the concept of positioning according to Ries & Trout. Because wherever some smart know-all marketer thinks he might be positioning a brand in the market, a really smart person knows that the exercize is incomplete unless that position has been reached in the prospect's mind.

To understand this, I ask you to consider two facts:

1. Think of how many brands there are in the category you are trying to win.

A study done a few years ago in the USA showed that there were over 10,000 products in the average supermarket. They showed that the 'hypermarkets' becoming slowly popular in the Western world can display between 30,000 to 50,000 products.

Taking just two categories at random in the industrial field, they found over 80,000 companies (of which 292 exclusively manufactured centrifugal pumps!).

They found 175 brands of cigarettes in the market.

Over 100,000 brands of prescription drugs! (How would you like to be the marketer that has to fight through *that* jungle for a niche in the doctor's mind?)

Medical studies show that the average consumer has *no trouble* with trying to remember all these competing products simply because *his brain does not even try!*

That's it. It switches off. Shuts down. A few products in the category are retained (if the category is important in the first place). And after that, it's goodbye. See ya later.

Just in case we were all talking at once, here's who said what and when. And what it was that you had the perspicacity to approve.

The Campaign Palace has been described as many things.
But never a registered charity.
So please send your cheque for the following invoice to: P.O. Box 134. Mosman. 2088.

The Campaign Palace is an advertising agency that puts as much effort into positioning itself as it does for its clients. Above are the letterheads it uses for all its contact reports and its bills.

Nobody buys much when they're asleep.

Our philosophy about advertising is simple.

Over-simplifying it, there are two kinds of advertising.

The dull, expected kind of advertising that you see every where, all the time.

It would seem that many agencies are very good at this.

Or the exciting, innovative kind of advertising that you see all too rarely.

Now we would be the first to admit that both are able to produce results, to a greater or lesser extent.

It's just that you need to spend far more money on the first to make it work.

And it's all so boring for the client, and the agency, and the consumer, that it ends up sending them all to sleep.

So, we prefer to concentrate on trying to produce the second kind.

The Campaign Palace are Accredited Advertising Agents with offices in Melbourne and Sydney.

Our Melbourne address is 409 St. Kilda Road, Melbourne, Victoria, 3004. P.O. Box 7101, 416 St. Kilda Road, Melbourne, Victoria, 3004, Australia.

Telephone (03) 267 7877.
Telex Marlin AA36559.
Facsimile (03) 267 5307.

The Campaign Palace.

This is the letterhead of The Campaign Palace (Australia). Every letter carries their philosophy.

Don't call us, we won't call you.

To illustrate this 'first-heard-best-remembered' principle, Ries and Trout have an interesting exercise: Can you name the first person to fly a plane? The first to land on the moon? The highest mountain range in the world?

Yes? Now name the second

Difficult, huh?

As they put it in their book "Positioning: The Battle for Your mind": "The first thing you need to indelibly fix your message in the mind is not the message, it's the mind." An innocent mind, untarnished in that category.

If you're ever going to take on a leader, or become one, it is best to remember this fact of life.

2. Now think of how many messages there are competing against yours in the world out there.

Think of radio, outdoor, TV, press, Point of Sale, matchbook covers, car badges, rear windows, and almost any surface that meets your eye as you look around right now.

Somebody, somewhere in your country, is talking to your customer about a competing brand (in your product category) *right now* as you read this article, through one medium or another.

And the customer is going to remember only one or two of these competing brands. So the odds are loaded in favor of the leader.

Another thing to remember if you are the leader (or plan to get there) is: The fact that you are the Number 1 selling brand will never serve more than as a reassurance for a pre-converted purchaser. *It will never be a primary reason to buy.*

It's much better if the consumer remembers you as the 'real thing' (Coke) or actually starts to name the category after you (Polaroid cameras and Xerox copiers).

It also means that your real power in the consumer's mind comes from your product, and not your company. If you are the leader, learn to react rapidly to the competition — you can afford to undercut, outpromote, defend your territory with 'covering brands' or change your company name to include broader fields if that is what the consumer knows about you in his mind.

In other words, keep your eyes and ears open all the time.

Following a leader

The one thing you don't do is go head-on, on Day One.

If the leader is selling himself on the fact that his widgets are bigger, the size of your widgets (big or small) is not going to matter at all.

Because the position called BIG WIDGETS in the consumer's mind is already occupied by your competitor and anything you say is simply going to remind him to buy from your competition.

Now, the trick is to find if there is a hole in the mind (and in the marketplace) for longer widgets or more reliable widgets. Then go and plug the heck out of that benefit.

Many years ago, Claude Hopkins was a copywriter who was asked to write ads for Bissell Carpet Cleaners. Since reliability and length (and almost every other competitive position) was already occupied by the competition, he broke with a campaign that said: *"We make carpet cleaners with handles that come in twelve different colours to suit your choice."*

This type of ingenuity deserved success, and Bissell, by staying single-minded, soon became Number One. More recently, when an almost unknown maker of Swedish cars came to Scali, McCabe and Sloves in New York, the creative partner, Ed McCabe, helped to position Volvo not as the best engineered car (Mercedes) or the most expensive car (Cadillac or Rolls) or the sportiest. He figured that the lawyers and doctors and respectable middle classes were probably ready for a safe and reliable car, and that's what his advertising said. Volvo soon gained a very respectable and profitable share of the imported market.

What these successes had in common was the ability to find the niche in the consumer's mind (and in the marketplace) and then the courage to stick to this position single mindedly over the years.

What all this really means is: even follow-the-leader can be a quite profitable game if you don't let the corporate ego get in the way.

Last 3 tips

Don't launch with a new product "just because you have the spare capacity in the factory." The consumer might not have spare capacity in his mind.

Don't dazzle the consumer with science. Too much input and the brain wipes out the program.

Don't try to be all things to all people: Be exact in your targetting.

People have different needs, desires, ambitions, self-concepts and perceptions. Cater to the specific audience, and your communication will be sharper.

The only retail store, for instance, that can afford to ignore this last rule is probably the Gum Store in Moscow.

But then, they don't have much competition over there.

Yet.

VII

Positioning a product in the marketplace (Part 3).

"The unleashed power of the atom has changed everything save our modes of thinking, and we thus drift toward unparallelled catastrophes."

- *Albert Einstein*

QUITE recently, I broke into a cold sweat during a meeting at my office.

My heart palpitated, my insides squirmed, and my toes curled as I heard those dreaded words from a client: "We have decided to go into line extensions."

(It reminds me of a movie I saw with the comedian, Steve Martin, who went into a paroxysm everytime he heard the word "cleaning woman" during the movie. It was so bizarre, it was funny.)

The problem I have is simple: If you are known in the market as the ultimate remedy for headaches, and they know and have trusted you for years as the ultimate headache cure — WHEN YOU OWN THE HEADACHE CURE POSITION IN THE CONSUMER'S MIND — why would you decide to jeopardise this leadership role — this well defined image — by trying to communicate to this over-communicated-to prospect that you now also make a great tummy-pain reliever under the same brand name?

Because now, you are asking the poor, over-burdened brain you are addressing to carry TWO bits of information about your alleged greatness: That you can help heads and tummies.

Hang on a minute. There is already somebody else in the tummy relief department of the prospect's mind. It could be Alka-Seltzer. It could be Eno. But whoever it is, it's not your brand. How anyone can possibly fly in the face of this logic (and many otherwise-savvy marketers consistently did this in the Seventies — leaving a gigantic problem for their successors in the Eighties) is a wonder to behold.

I have plugged the Ries & Trout book on positioning so massively these last two chapters, they should send me a cheque soon! But I'll give you another example that they used to illustrate this problem a few years ago.

Leading marketers of Dial Deodorant Soap decided to market a Dial Deodorant (i.e., without the soap), and the marketers of Bayer, the people who "invented" aspirin decided to attack the "anti-aspirin" approach of Tylenol with "Bayer non-aspirin pain reliever". This, of course, before the recent studies claiming the beneficial aspects of analgesics!

Well, the battle ended with Dial still with a large share of the deodorant soap market and a very, very small share of the deodorant market.

And Bayer's non-aspirin failed to make much headway in the acetaminophen market.

These are but two of a multitude of examples. Of course, there are marketers who will still argue with both sides of the toss. The defenders of the line extension strategy, no doubt, will say: "Well, perhaps the perception of Dial's overall deodorant qualities was strengthened by its foray into the pure deodorant market," and so on.

And who knows, maybe it's true. After all what's in a name?

Plenty, according to Messrs. Ries & Trout. The example they use is Proctor & Gamble. As a house name, it is unknown to consumers. But Colgate-Palmolive used to field a plethora of house names: — Colgate Dental Cream, Colgate Instant Shave, Colgate 100 Oral powder, Palmolive Liquid Detergent, Palmolive Rapid Shave, Palmolive Shaving Cream and Palmolive Soap.

P&G, on the other hand, fields names which have no connection with the company name: Tide, Cheer, Bold, etc.

And yet, P&G did twice the business and made three times the profit than Colgate-Palmolive in the year of the survey, with fewer brands!

Again, it could be argued that Colgate-Palmolive was right to use house names because the names were a real property because of their history in the marketplace (and in the prospect's mind), but it is difficult to argue with figures.

When Xerox, well known for making copiers, went into the computer business under the same brand name, it wrote off $84.4 million in losses.

And IBM, well known for its computers, did not do too well with its line of plain paper copiers.

Marketers who regard their name as a safety net instead of a living tool to be hammered and burnished to gleaming victory, often get what they deserve.

You can wave your corporate ego when you like, but you can't argue with history. And history is written every year in different colors of ink in annual reports. Look them up.

They are public property.

But to me, the essence of the argument against line extension is the fact that it destroys the charisma, the mystique of the mother brand. It destroys the illusion that the original name is the original product — that Bayer is almost a generic for aspirin, a superior form of aspirin.

Because you lose more than mere perceptions when you lose something like that.

You lose a corner.

Of somebody's mind.

VIII

Are you paying too little for your TV production?

AND WE COULD SAVE
ANOTHER $10 BY
CATCHING THE BUS TO
THE SHOOT.

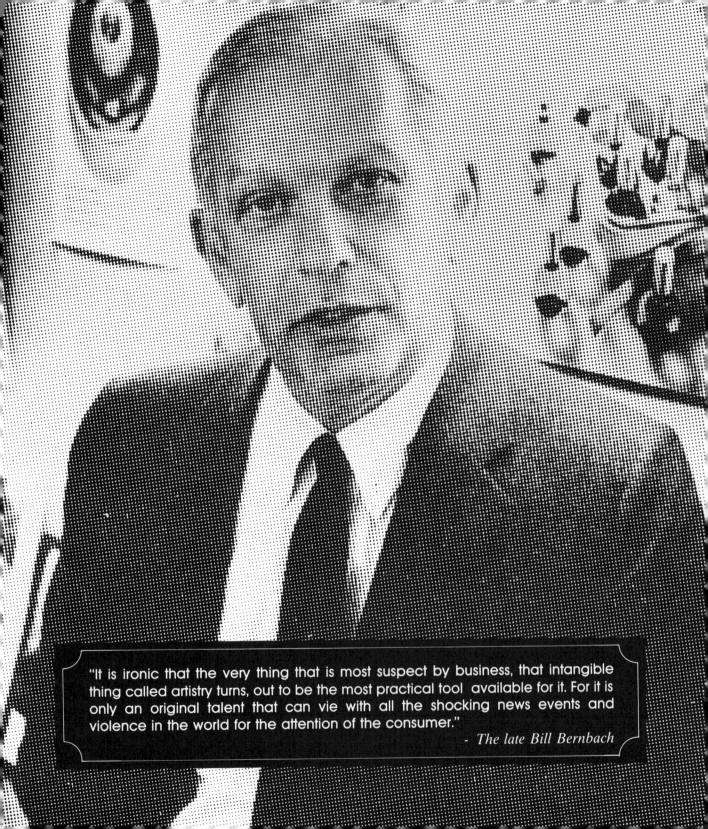

"It is ironic that the very thing that is most suspect by business, that intangible thing called artistry turns, out to be the most practical tool available for it. For it is only an original talent that can vie with all the shocking news events and violence in the world for the attention of the consumer."

- The late Bill Bernbach

D

o yourself a favor.

Settle down. Relax. Now please read the Bill Bernbach quote on the previous page one more time before you read this chapter. Because this quote applies equally to the qualities you must look for in your advertising as well as TV production.

Have you read it again?

So, now we both know where we stand. You distrust artistry, Mr Businessman, and you want to slash TV production costs, and I am going to show you where you can slash them, but mostly where you can't. Let me explain how, every time you think you are saving money, you are out-smarting yourself.

You are actually *losing* money. By the bucketload.

Before we talk about TV production, let's talk about the medium.

I mean, when you have finally produced this great low-cost commercial, it is going to appear somewhere, right? On television, right? And that's not cheap, is it?

So, how do you go about booking your ad?

You spend a lot of time getting the right time slots. You make sure (or your agency media planner makes sure) that your ads will appear at the lowest cost per thousand for the greatest number of people in your target group. Now, the commercial might cost you only, for example, $40,000 to produce. Over the life of that campaign, using this 'low cost' commercial, you will spend, say $400,000, which is the cost of buying the time on the TV stations which will broadcast your commercial.

So you say to yourself: "What if I spend $30,000 on the production of this TV ad, and use the savings to get more time, more insertions, on the TV stations? Or, perhaps, buy my son a new car?"

Well, if advertising was a business exactly like any other, your thinking would be absolutely correct. A dollar saved is a dollar earned. "It is profit that will look great to the shareholders at the end of the day," you say. How right you are.

And how wrong.

Because now I want you to digest four facts that will help you to look at the same scenario in another way:

1. You know a lot about what you manufacture.

2. You know a lot about the kind of people who buy your product.

3. Your media planner knows a lot about how to get the best program on the best channel which gives you the maximum number of people, who actually *need* your product, watching your commercial in the right frame of mind.

59

4. But you don't know anything about making TV commercials.

(Or at least, you don't know as much as the director, the producer, the casting head, the wardrobe person, the make-up person, the lighting people, the camera man, the prop expert, the model maker and you certainly have not made as many commercials as the agency that is recommending all of these to you in the first place.)

Now, assuming that you are dealing with good, honest people (and most of them are, or you should switch to working with people you can trust — get an advertising partner relationship instead of a master-servant relationship) where do you think your saving of $10,000 is going to come from?

It is going to come from bad casting, unimaginative directors, shonky cameramen, cheap film stock, tacky wardrobes, bad lighting and inefficient film crews.

So now you have saved $10,000, but you have a cheap TV production. And there is one inflexible rule about cheap productions: They look cheap.

Your advertising, Mr Businessman, is your public face to the world.

And cheap-looking productions make your product or your service or whatever it is you are trying to sell, look cheap.

Now, if you go back to where we started, here is your ad, running to the maximum number of people in the best possible media buy, and it is telling the world that you are cheap. Your product is cheap. Your service is cheap. It is like putting on your cheapest, threadbare suit just when you are about to address the maximum number of people at your daughter's wedding.

The $10,000 you saved could eventually cost you untold millions in lost sales, lost image. Lost opportunities. Gone. Forever.

Think of it this way: Media effectiveness is inversely proportionate to the shoddiness of your commercial. The more people you reach in your target group with a bad commercial, the quicker they find out about your bad image.

All this, of course, is not to say that you need expensive commercials to be effective in the marketplace. What you really need is truth, honesty and great ideas. But if you find that a commercial you have approved is, in fact, too expensive for your budget, don't cut down that same idea just to meet your cost everytime. In the USA, the land of the million dollar production, I wrote a commercial two years ago for a regional client that cost only $750. But it ended up free, as a part of the prime time regional news slots of CBS & NBC. It had a big idea instead of a big budget and the free PR made it worth a million bucks anyway.

Because a commercial (like an idea) is going to cost what it is going to cost. No more. No less. If it is too expensive for your pocket, ask for, and you shall receive, a new idea.

You can't have your cake and eat it, too. Except in fantasy. Or in film stories.
Or TV commercials.
And TV commercials cost money.

IX

How to get more out of your ad agency.

"Leadership is intangible, and therefore no weapon ever designed can replace it."

- General Omar Bradley

**IF the client moans and sighs,
Make his logo twice the size.
If he still should prove refractory,
Stick in a picture of his factory.
Only in the direct cases,
Should you insert the client's faces."**

Or, as The Rolling Stones used to say: "You can't always get what you want. You get what you need."

But now, you are getting what you *think* you need.

A bigger logo of your company? A picture of your factory?

Come on, don't tell me you've never been tempted. Especially that one about the logo. Or, maybe, a bigger pack than the agency wanted to give your last ad.

Well, we've all been known to want some crazy things in our lifetimes. But how many times have you *told* the ad agency to do it.

And why not? After all, it's your money that is paying for the ad. You have every right to tell the ad agency where to stick the, er, ah, your logo.

Just like you have every right to tell your doctor what your disease is. And what he should write on your prescription. Or to tell your lawyer how to plan the strategies to fight your next case.

But you don't do that because you don't know enough about medicine or law. You feel, however, that you know more about advertising. Isn't that the stuff you see in the papers and on the telly every day? Naturally, you know as much as we do.

And that, of course, is precisely the sort of attitude that gave rise to the bit of doggerel with which I started this chapter today. The old timers knew how to survive the whims and fancies of domineering clients. The 'bigger logo' formula often kept the wolf from their door. Who needs ulcers everyday?

And many of the 'old timers' are still around.

Oh, they look pretty young.

A snazzy-suited, sharp-talking, young account executive or fading creative has-been will lie down and whimper these days just as quickly as they used to in the days of yore. And the only person who loses will be you because, like I said before, it is your money that is buying the advertising. And if it's less effective because the message got lost in the clutter (because your logo or your factory or your face got in the way), hey, too bad. Your problem. You called the shots, remember?

"Victory is the main object of war," said Sun Tzu in The Art of War: *"If this is long delayed, weapons are blunted and morale depressed."* This is as true today as it was all those centuries ago. Now, when you hire an agency to fight for you, our morale can become blunted if you constantly tell granny how to suck eggs. When you appoint a team of professionals, they are as human and as ready to give it their best as any soldier at the dawn of battle. Constant interference from people who have dedicated their lives to *making* widgets instead of *advertising* widgets can end up in a relationship where the agency is often too willing to give you bigger logos and widget factory shots instead of great, persuasive, telegraphic, dramatic and memorable advertising.

And because you don't know as much about advertising as we do, you might never know the difference. Think about that.

"Clients," the saying goes, "get the advertising they deserve."

A bigger logo and pack is easy, for instance, but there are no free lunches. Anything that is bigger makes something else smaller. And that 'something else' might well turn out to be the message, or the relevant device you needed to get attention in the first place.

I am not, for one moment, espousing smaller logos and miniscule packs. I am simply saying that to get the biggest bang out of your advertising dollar, appoint good people and let them get on with it. On average, they are as dedicated to their business, to excellence, as you or I. No more, no less.

But, to go back to 'getting the most out of your ad agency', consider the following rules. They just might help you turn your supplier of words and pictures and film and sound into something worth infinitely more — a business partner with great ideas that make money:

1. *The agency knows more about advertising than you do.*
As David Ogilvy used to say: *"Don't keep a dog and bark yourself."* Get a good agency and get out of the way. I can think of no famous, effective campaign that was re-written by the client, or after client interference. Of course, there are a few exceptions that prove the rule, but when you think of, say, "Avis we try harder" or "Volkswagen Think Small" or "Heineken refreshes the parts other beers cannot reach" or "At 60 mph the loudest noise in a Rolls Royce is the ticking of the electric clock" (and I could go on till the next page), you are looking at example after example of immortal ads that had

I DON'T CARE IF IT WILL DEVELOP GREATER COMPLEXITY WITH AGE. I HAVE TO BE BACK AT THE OFFICE BY 2:36.

OF COURSE IT'S A GREAT RHINE RIESLING. BUT WHY TALK ABOUT IT WHEN YOU COULD BE DRINKING IT

Another Australian ad, probably written by a copywriter in a rush to get back to his agency to work harder for you.

clients with the wisdom and perspicacity to inspire ad agencies to great heights by leaving them well enough alone.

2. *Trust your ad agency.*

A client/ad agency relationship is like any successful marriage. Don't tell us all your secrets, but most of them. Or at least the ones you think can help us do a better job for you. Advertising is full of business people as honest and as responsible as you. Sure, the relationship might end one day. But you can't start a marriage by thinking of divorce. If we are going to be disseminating information about you, we are going to ask for access to more information about you than you think we need.

Would you ask your doctor to use his stethoscope without opening your shirt?

3. *Don't set impossible deadlines.*

I once challenged Helmut Korne, a great New York adman who was responsible for some of the ads mentioned in Rule One above, why he had not done anything great lately. Instead of upbraiding me for my impertinence, he humbled me by giving my question serious consideration and said: "Avis and Volkswagen were breakthroughs. You can't come in every Monday and say, Aha!, I think I'll have a breakthrough!". Breakthroughs take time. At the heart of every great ad is a great original idea. And original ideas don't always keep to your timetable.

4. *Encourage differences of opinion.*

We, your agency, take our lives into our hands every time we tell you that you are wrong (well, our business life, anyway, is at risk!). And how many businessmen do you know whose business often means having to tell the customer he is wrong?

Or look at it this way: Do you really need an ad agency that always tells you that you are right? When you hire an agency, it has no stock to sell you but its brains. Encourage them to use that grey matter and it will do more than expand your business. It will expand your horizons.

Add one champagne

5. *Agencies are full of human beings.*

Real people. People with hopes and aspirations and dreams and tears and laughter. And if these people, occasionally, do something right and good and great, praise them to the skies. Recently, a client sent me a bottle of Dom Perignon after I had written the campaign. It was you might say, a small gift. But it was a great vintage! And I'll work all the harder for the thought behind the gesture.

You don't have to open the bubbly every time we get a good idea, but a pat on the back goes a long way.

I have found that advertising people work much harder for things other than money. Awards, peer group approval, praise, or the sheer stubborn obsession about beating their own last ad with a better one.

But, ahem, don't stop the money, please. It all helps, you know!

X

Research: Final judge or fool's gold?

RESEARCH PROVES
50% OF MEN AND 10% OF WOMEN
WILL BUY THIS PRODUCT.

"Logistics is the ball and chain of armored warfare."

- *Heinz Guderain*

R

ESEARCH, like love, can come in all shapes and sizes.

And, like flatulence, it can come at you quite suddenly.

I mean, you could be sitting there quite innocently at your next agency meeting, trying to evaluate an ad and bang, out of nowhere, you could have this trusted team of elite professionals trying to dazzle you with science.

Because now we've got all kinds of research to throw at you.

There is research for finding out what flavor your targets will like when you finally decide on your next line of edible widgets. There is research that can tell what name the world will like. There's research that will tell you how to talk to your target audience. Research that can tell you whether the ad will be liked. Or seen. Or remembered. There is research that even pretends it can tell you if the ad will launch your product or sell it in the marketplace.

(That last one is the funniest claim of all, considering that seven out of ten new products die in the marketplace, and yet all of them are heavily researched before they are launched.)

There is research that *thinks* it can tell you which politician will win the presidential race. Research that tries to tell you whether your ad was seen and heard last night. (This is a good one, too. Many ads that do well in the 'seen and heard' section die miserably in the marketplace! Because the canny housewife can *see* an ad and *hear* it and even *tell* the dedicated researcher that she likes the ad for Brand X but, come shopping day, she cheerfully goes back to her habit of buying Brand Y.)

Research that promises you all this, and heaven too, is simply taking you for a ride, using your research dollars for fuel.

Because research that makes such wild promises is taking the consumer for granted. And any marketer with common sense will tell you that this is a dangerous thing.

To me, the consumer has always been a bit like the fickle, equivocating Casca in Shakespeare's Julius Caesar. When Cassius asked Casca if he would come to his home for dinner, the reply he got was something like *"Aye, if thy mind hold, the weather be good and the dinner be worth the eating."*

Research cannot predict consumer behavior, any more than a soothsayer can predict the future from the innards of a goat. Heck, even the modern weathermen, with their hi-tech gizmos and ultra-modern radars and their high-flying satellites, can often make a mistake in predicting tomorrow's temperature. It's naive in the extreme for a marketer to suppose that a bunch of housewives around a table can tell him whether his product will be the next hit on the supermarket shelf. Or whether the ad his agency has created is going to motivate these same ladies to actually pay hard-earned money for the product when they see it. Because liking an ad in a "research" environment is not quite the same as parting with money and breaking lifelong habits.

So, where did these misconceptions about research come from? Certainly, not the research companies. In fact, most respectable research companies are often at pains to point out what their research cannot do for you. The preambles to research documents that arrive after the study has been conducted often go out of their way to say that what you are about to read are only indications that should be used as pointers, rather than edicts carved in stone.

Recently, the head of a very famous research company in this region — and the techniques they use here are often as modern and reliable as any other part of the world — told me that his favourite quote was (another Ogilvyism!): *"Most people use research like a drunk uses a lamp post: more for support than illumination."*

And 'support' is the key word in this statement. In companies run by middle-level mediocrities rather than owner-management decision-makers of the old days, support is a highly prized commodity when you want to pass the buck. Or, as the Americans say, cover your behind.

A chief executive officer often understands that there is no such thing as a sure thing. And that he is paid to make decisions that are, often, no surer of success than any normal entrepreneurial decision can be. Intelligent risk-taking is the name of the game.

Research, usually, can do no more than light the path way to good decision-making. If it was a 100% guarantee to success, everyone with a research budget and an interview clipboard would become a millionaire overnight.

Another misconception: 'creative people don't like research'. Once, in Australia, in the first year that I managed to gain more than my fair share of awards and peer group ratings, I was invited to speak in a debate about the benefits and failures of research. I declined, because the organizers automatically assumed that "all creatives are against research." In actual fact, I did, and still do, rely more heavily on research than almost anyone I know, to guide my path as I grope for solutions.

I later found that this is also true for some of the best creative people in the world! But they use research to generate ideas, not to judge them.

Research can be a fascinating window into the lives of consumers when you are trying to create an ad or plan strategy. It can open up their minds and hearts to us, their likes and dislikes, their language and the vocabulary that they use as they go about their everyday existence. Research, used as a tool, in almost any aspect of marketing, can help decision-making more than any other reference point that I can think of.

It can put an army at your fingertips.

It can help improve your product or service every year because you enter into a dialogue with the consumer and she constantly tells what she likes and doesn't like, and when the competitor is offering a deal that is better than yours.

Research, used thus, as a continuous process of listening and upgrading, can help you stay on your toes.

Advertisers nowadays want more from their ad agencies than just clever puns, hi-gloss visuals and funny headlines. They want effective advertising that more than makes a witty point. They are demanding advertising that makes *money*. Because more of them are beginning to see how it can instantly make a major difference to their profits in many product categories. That is why we are given more and more flexibility to use research that builds ideas. And many creative people are taking to it with enthusiasm.

The other day, at a meeting with a client interested in exploring the possibilities of a new kind of product, one of my creative group heads disputed something that was said. When asked how he knew better, he said that he had recently taken 12 examples of the new product to his housing area, distributed six to maids and six to housewives, and then taken the trouble to visit each of them again to tabulate their response!

I don't know what you think, but in my book, that is a kid who will go far in this or any other business.

So, research. Final judge or fool's gold?

Well, if you're going to use research intelligently, don't ask me.

You decide.

XI
Media: Impact, or frequency?

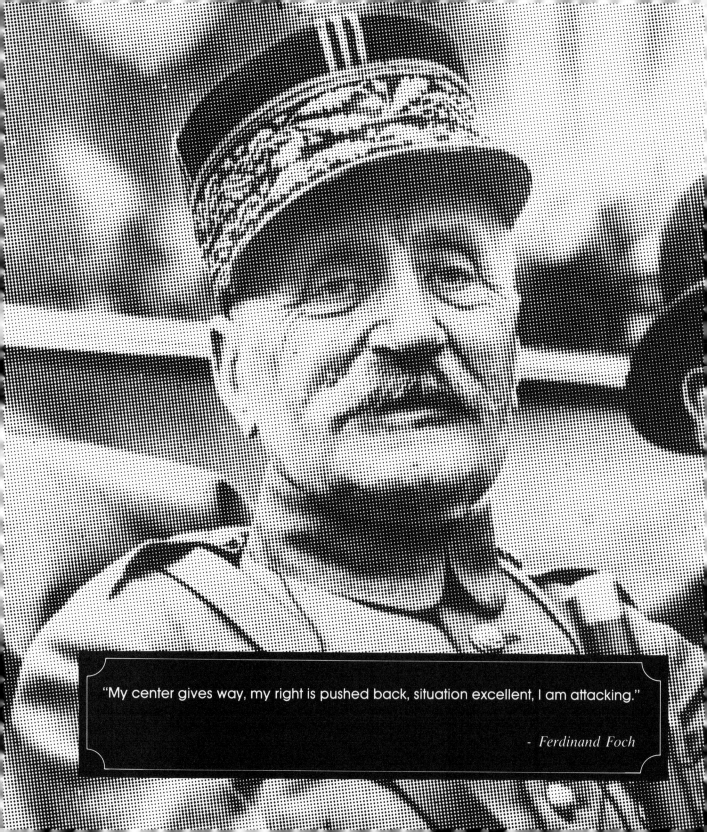

"My center gives way, my right is pushed back, situation excellent, I am attacking."

- *Ferdinand Foch*

I've never been a darling of media directors.

Oh, I like them. I like media planners, and buyers and bookers and time and space sales teams and all those people who look like they do nothing but play with their computers all day.

That's where my money comes from. (In fact, when the advertising business first began, ad agencies were basically commission agents who just acted as brokers between the advertiser and the newspapers.)

If there were no media people, there would be no creative people.

So, initially, when I met a media person, we would get along just fine. They were always gratified that some creative person was taking an interest in their department. They would swell with joy when I said things like "media planning is as creative as writing ads."

Things only got shaky when they found out that I really meant what I said. That media planning should go hand in hand, and side by side, with the process of creating ads. They sometimes acted less than amused when I tried to create sizes that were different from the usual half or quarter page formats. Or tried to buy two 10-seconders back to back for the same product. Or a commercial in two parts where one was the last one in a commercial break. And the second commercial completed a story that the first one began by becoming the first commercial in the following commercial break. Or when an outdoor boarding was left deliberately incomplete to emphasise a specific aspect of the product's promise. Or when I wrote a radio campaign that included the live involvement of 24 disc jockeys in a specific section of a pre-recorded commercial, in 24 separate radio stations across the country, simultaneously.

These problems reduce, of course, when one is executive creative director and on the board of the agency. But I often talk to creative people who are trying to do something different and end up having the system beat them down. And when I come across such examples in the industry, I try to encourage disagreement and diversity of views.

I do this because the people who create the ads are as much 'the system' as the people who book the time and the space for those ads to appear.

I am writing down all this because, while trying to get different opinions on the subject of *"Media: Impact or frequency?"* the reply I got most often when I spoke to people was: "It depends on the ad. Is it a 10-second or a 30? Is it small space or full page?"

This point of view depressed me terribly. Because it meant that in many ad agencies not only was the tail wagging the dog, but that this was seen to be an acceptable state of affairs! It made the subject a sort of non-question because most people did not even see the need to seriously examine this situation.

The other day, I spoke with Bruce Baldwin, my old art director who did the cartoons in this book and who now works for The Campaign Palace, the advertising agency that produces the most innovative advertising in Australia. On the subject of media, he talked about his first project with Lionel Hunt, the copywriter who founded the agency. As my friend opened his layout pad to make the first rough for the ad, Mr Hunt reached across and turned the pad from a vertical to a horizontal position, thereby automatically turning the ad, *which still hadn't been created,* from a single full page to a double full page spread in the newspaper.

He was talking impact.

When Apple Computers decided to position themselves as different to the IBM clones, Chiat & Day, their ad agency, created a two-minute commercial for only one insertion during the U.S. Superbowl (the most expensive TV buy in world history because the ad was never meant to run again) and set off their company into a national mindset that probably pays off today in ways that you can never quantify.

They were talking impact.

When a soft-drink company in Hong Kong decided to use "roadblocking" as a media technique, they made a two-minute commercial that appeared on all four TV stations at exactly the same time! This way, among other advantages of impact, even the remote control that some viewers use (commercial zapping) to browse around the stations during a commercial break was useless in the hands of a canny media planner working hand-in-hand with a good client contract and creative team.

They were talking impact.

Because that is what advertising is: impact! In fact, many decades ago, when a couple of guys called Messrs. Young and Rubicam on Madison Avenue decided to advertise their own business to prospective clients with their definition of what advertising really is, they used a blowup of a face with a fist landing on its chin, below a one-word headline. And do you know what that one-word headline said, above this face of a negro boxer with a fist landing on his chin? Just these six letters: I-M-P-A-C-T!

No so many years ago, an agro-chemical company that was also into pharmaceuticals and medical equipment and goodness knows what else, wanted to tell the world about itself. Instead of dribs and drabs of little corporate ads (corporate ads, often, are just another name for self-manipulation), they decided to blow their entire year's budget in one issue of The Times. They simply booked every single available full page in the newspaper. Aha, you say, but was the advertising successful? I asked the same question of the account executive on the English project. Here is his answer: *"Successful? All I can say is that we went on to repeat the same exercise in Europe the next year by booking every full page in one issue of the Frankfurter Allgemeine Zeitung and then, later, in Le Figaro."* The name of the advertiser was Fisons.

The ads were effective, because they were talking impact.

So, what should you do with the media budget? Go for frequency (that is, lots of ads, not necessarily prime time or Page Three, that are spread out over the year and look like neat, orderly little crosses on your media planners sheet)? Or should you go for bursts and short flights with impact and energy that turns the media planner's sheet into a dynamic document, geared for reaching the maximum number of people in such a way that you dominate the medium on that day?

Perhaps I have made too strong a case for impact over frequency, but I feel I need to do this. The pendulum has swung over too far the other way. Advertising by numbers seems to be the trend rather than the initiative and specific-case-thinking that is necessary when it comes to media planning.

There is a case to make for the other side. But I just don't want the planners who run their departments 'on autopilot' to nickel and dime great ideas to death.

To be fair to them (The Frequency Freaks), you don't really need immediate awareness when you are selling a brand that is consumed on a daily basis by the mass of the market, if it already enjoys a high market share. You need, instead, to maintain top-of-mind awareness over an extended period of time. You need frequency. But when you think of it, by their very nature, these products are few and far between.

For the general run of advertising, it would seem to me, it is time we took a more objective view of creating and buying ads for impact instead of saving this just for product launches where you need to build awareness fast. We should use impact buying for re-launches and seasonal products and also for cases where the advertising is trying to say something truly new and unique about the product or for that matter, about the consumer who uses it.

I still remember a T-shirt I once saw at a Ford Dealers-Ad Agency Conference in Melbourne, which said "Grab' em by the balls, and their hearts and minds will follow."

Now, that's impact.

XII

Public relations and paid advertising.

"War is the realm of chance. No other human activity gives it greater scope, no other has such incessant and varied dealings with this intruder. Chance makes everything more uncertain and interferes with the whole course of events."

- *Karl Von Clausewitz*

BELIEVE it or not, the two are not terribly different.

Public relations does not mean just sending a press release and a couple of 5″ × 7″ photographs to the local paper and hoping for the best.

If your company is faced with a serious problem, or a negative image, public relations could mean taking quick action and *being seen* to be taking quick action.

A crisis, for instance, like the Union Carbide tragedy in Bihar, India, that resulted in the loss of over 2,000 lives.

New Wave PR people have a name for it. They call it "crisis control," and they have lots of new books and theories on how to achieve it.

Sometimes, drastic action, decisive action, is at the heart of "crisis control." Probably the best example in recent times was the action taken by Johnson & Johnson in America when a few bottles of Tylenol were discovered to have been poisoned by some demented miscreant. Instead of trying to stonewall the situation (like the Russians at Chernobyl who insisted nothing had happened even after radioactive gases had started on their way to Europe), Johnson & Johnson simply withdrew their entire stock of Tylenol from the U.S. market at horrendous cost to themselves! But the crisis passed, and their decisive action turned out to be a priceless investment in their good name and reputation, and an action that stands them in good stead up to today.

The common factor between public relations and paid advertising is that both try to influence your target audience in what they say and think about you. In the worst case, it could be to stop them saying bad things about you. In the best, it could encourage them to say good things about you. And buy your product or service.

And since a business lives its life, by varying degrees, in the public eye, truth will usually come out. Which means that whatever it is you are trying to say, and to get people to say about you, has to be legal and just and honest or it will only come back to haunt you in the end. For instance, if your morning paper were to claim higher circulation figures than it really has, it would eventually lose credibility with media buyers. Or if you make a claim in your advertising and your public relations releases that is either untrue or vastly exaggerated, it can cost even more money in the long run.

Or, in the short run. Consider this: You invent a better mousetrap. Let's say it is a chemical mousetrap.

You decide to advertise it. But you have spent a lot of money in its manufacture and, maybe, you've got your whole business riding on it. So, you give in to the temptation of insisting that your advertising agency claims that it can also catch roaches.

NO.

No.

It is supposed to be the hardest word in the public relations business.

But at Presko, the largest pr firm in Southeast Asia, we've been using it for 28 years. We say "no" to press releases without substance or meat, or any pr programme without strategy or carefully thought out planning. We say "no", if we disagree, to blue chip clients like Citibank, Lufthansa, Seiko, Boeing, and Amway, and they respect us for it.

We believe that a client does not need a pr consultant if all that the consultant is going to do is agree with everything the client says. The best strategies are born through a partnership of ideas. At Presko we work with our clients towards convictions instead of compromises.

So, if you're looking to make a career in public relations, and you feel you can enjoy dealing with people in all types of businesses from aircraft and aspirin to hairspray or high government office or, in fact, almost any industry you can think of, write today in the strictest confidence to our chairman, Mr. Esko Pajasalmi, and find out why so many clients say "yes" to Presko. Our address is PRESKO Limited, GPO Box 1651, Bangkok 10501.

The training you get could get you to the top. In this, or any other business.

PRESKO

This classified ad that Raj Marwah wrote for a Thai PR company got them congratulatory letters from their competitors: Shandwick in London, IPR in Tokyo and Hill & Knowlton in Hong Kong. Each is the largest in its own market.

You even get some rough studies that allow you to get away with that claim. The advertising runs, and people flock to buy your product. The product is a hit, it is rolling off the retail shelves and more people are buying it than ever bought a mousetrap in the first week of introduction than ever before. And the day after they install it, they discover that it traps mice alright, but not the cockroaches. In fact, they find that the cockroaches are having a party in there, come morning.

Quite simply, that's where your overclaim starts to work against you. Your product dies as fast as it rose.

Suddenly, because more people have bought your story, more people have heard and seen and remembered your story — more people *don't* like your product any more! They tell their friends and relatives who turn away from your product in droves. Week Two rolls around and now nobody is buying your product. It sits there on the shelves, collecting dust. And cockroaches.

Fortunately, there is new breed of PR people who like to say 'no' to clients as often as they say 'yes'. Hasan Basar, an Oxford graduate who is one of the people helping to quietly change the face of public relations at Presko, one of Asia's premier PR outfits, puts it this way:

> **Because some people cannot gauge the impact they can get for their PR dollar, they tend to divide into two categories: those who think PR is a lot of hot air, and others who thinks it is so magical it creates presidents like Ronald Reagan. To my thinking, especially for the latter group who are usually approaching PR for the first time, my job is often to under-promise, to de-mythify. PR, or the changing of public attitudes to a person or corporation or product, is a slow process. It is the truth, properly reflected. It is more a gentle insistence, a slow dawning rather than overnight impact in a half page spread. In fact, what I usually say is, the moment people say someone's PR is working, it isn't. Because people tend to dig in with their old beliefs when they feel someone is trying to change their attitudes.**

A corporation can get caught with its foot in its own mousetrap just as often as a person who, for instance, shoots his mouth off at parties. Press releases full of puffery are routinely ignored or brutally edited by the media. A senior journalist from a leading paper confessed to me the other day that he would value press releases much more if they would obey two golden rules:

1. Send them out less often (that is, only when what you have to say is genuinely newsworthy).

2. Reduce puffery. Cut it down by half.

In paid advertising, the rules of brevity and honesty are not all that different. Look carefully. There probably *is* a dramatic and honest and original claim you can make about your product. You just have to dig harder to find it. To paraphrase Robin Wight, the amazing chairman of WCRS Advertising, *"Interrogate a product till it confesses its promise."*

To the two rules of PR above, I would like to add a third — one of my own:

3. When in doubt, take the hard option. Take the high road.

Because the bigger your size in the market, the more likely it is that you will be a target of one kind of attack or another. In these circumstances, honesty is more than a moral imperative — it is a policy for survival in a competitive world.

Let me give you one final, personal example. One Saturday, I was invited to sit and judge, with a jury of my peers, advertising worthy of awards at an 'Art Directors Association'. Since it is a serious attempt to get advertising judged by the people who actually create it, I was happy to participate. The organizers sensibly started with an admonition that none of us vote on advertising created by the agency that each of us represented.

This threw me in a quandary. Since I had been in the country just five months, I could not hope to recognise every single one of the ads created by my agency the previous year. I knew that if I kept quiet, I'd probably recognize about 95% of them — but I ran the risk of voting on a few of my own agency's ads, and that was contrary to the rules.

Instead, I took a deep breath and admitted to the gathering that I would not be able to recognize all the ads created by the vast organization I represented!

Imagine my relief when people rushed over to help me go through the entire list and kept helping me right through the judging.

A couple of people laughed. But I made quite a few new friends that day.

If a person can react quickly, why can't a corporation?

I'll tell you why: Corporations are run by management groups and committees and, as one anonymous British scientist once said during the war:

❝ A committee is a cul-de-sac where good ideas are lured and quietly strangled. ❞

Unfortunately, PR as well as advertising is adjudicated upon by diverse groups who each *have* to make a point to justify their existence.

Personally, I'd rather present to a garden of vegetables than to such a group.

At least broccoli cannot *talk.*

XIII

The Doubting Thomases of Advertising.

"To be prepared for war is one of the most effective means of preserving the peace."

- George Washington

THESE Doubting Thomases come in three groups, and I don't know which irritates me most.

So this chapter is a blast at all of them.

First, there are the people who know absolutely nothing about advertising, and yet make snide remarks about our business all the time. You've met them at parties. They quote from bizarre, paranoid books like "Subliminal Advertising" and think that our office corridors are full of glamorous models, and secretaries who *want* to be glamorous models, killing time between wild orgies on weekends with the rich and famous.

And then there is the second group of people who are already in advertising, but are so young and impressionable, they accept this shallow and unreal role model reinforcement from TV and movie scripts written by people in the first group. They live their lives in a sort of hazy, ambivalent limboland, waiting to grow up so they can join Group Three.

And this one is the most unfortunate of all.

These are people who have such fat salaries in advertising they do not know what they are getting paid to do. Any moment now, they think, somebody will find that this is all a sham — or that generics or "home brands" or "home-based computer buying" will replace their jobs — and they will be out there, forced into 'the real world, selling widgets door-to-door.'

In some countries, there are actual groups with research funds and grants whose business is to generate arguments to defend advertising against vigilante bodies who have nothing to do with their time except to criticize one or another facet of advertising.

To my mind, having to defend advertising is a bit like defending the flag: sometimes essential, but it shouldn't really be necessary. Here is what I wrote on this subject for B&T, an Australian magazine, a few years ago. It is just as true today:

"I happen to think we've been getting just too bloody defensive about our industry in the last two decades.

I mean, if free enterprise is the name of the system, and the merchants and traders the engine, then advertising is the combustion: the fuel and the good oil that turns the cogs. And if the system has brought prosperity and better standards of living, it is because the trader or merchant had the guts to take a punt, by putting his shirt on his product. On research and development, on advertising.

Today, research has taken the gamble out of most elements in the marketing mix. But advertising is still a chemical reaction, totally dependent on the expertise of the chemist. It is the diagnosis and the remedy that is still as good as the knowledge of the doctor; the brief as good as the last barrister.

Advertising is the heart of the machine that makes the world go round. Without the freedom to advertise, we could well join the swelling grey ranks of Muscovites waiting outside GUM for the next shipment of bananas and bread, lemon and potatoes." (According to a recent piece in *Izvestia*, the Moscow housewife spends an average of 11 hours a week waiting in queues just to do her shopping!)

"Today, advertising has been lobbied and legislated enough to have put its own house in order. Self, or government, regulation in most countries has already made absolutely certain that the claims we make today are honest and true and fair and not harmful to health.

Commercialism isn't crass. It's healthy.

If some people criticize advertising, it is because they are misinformed about the essence of the freedom it represents. And if you feel advertising needs defending, don't just sit there with your graphs and charts. Attack!

If you are overburdened with research dollars and foundation grants, spend them instead on stemming the tide of ratbags and the whingeing fringe who speak for no one, represent nobody, and yet get unfairly equal space in some media.

Stop worrying so much about ads that are "insulting to the intelligence" or "in poor taste" or "offensive". The consumer in the open marketplace will sort out the bad 'uns by simply not buying the product that comes in rude colors.

Oh, and one more thing. Stop worrying about brand loyalties that might be swamped by a sea of generics or how the consumer will want the bare price and nothing else. Or that push-button purchasing will phase out the Artist of the Soft Sell.

There have always been brands with loyalties. And there have always been generics. For every Christ, there were a thousand generic prophets. For every Maharishi, a thousand generic gurus.

In an incredibly prescient remark on the eternal values of human nature, Dr Johnson once said: **"Promise, large promise, is the soul of an advertisement."**

"I'm not here to sell you a few pipes and boilers and vats," said Dr Johnson (a great writer of his time, and, like Marlowe, a part-time copywriter of leaflets and brochures!) when invited to auction off a local brewery. **"I'm here to sell you the opportunity to get rich beyond the dreams of avarices."**

Dreams. Whatever the future holds, there will be dreamers then as there are now. And people to sell dreams. And people who buy them.

A vendor should have the right to sell, and consumer to buy, the sizzle as well as the steak. And they will, no matter what the medium may be, no matter what the rules may be. Brand loyalties will blossom. New products, new media, and new means of selling them.

So let us not cower or run or hide from this new technology. Enjoy it. Embrace it. Celebrate it.

It just might set us free. **"**

XIV

How to kill a creative idea.

"A single death is a tragedy, a million deaths are a statistic."

Joseph Stalin

BEFORE all my creative colleagues stand up and applaud the fact that I am finally addressing the greatest creative problem of all time, I must acknowledge a debt to Rapp & Collins, a great international direct response company that thought up most of the 99 idea-killers you are about to read.

I simply changed a few, dropped a few, and added a few.

But if you have ever been involved in a creative enterprise of any kind, you've probably endured the incredible frustration of having to hear one of the lines printed below.

The sad fact is, the greatest talent in the world can die unread and unpublished, unproduced, unless there is someone who recognizes and buys the idea in the first place.

So if you're an idea killer, maybe you'll find a few lines in here you can use yourself.

And if you are, like me, trying to remain an idea *generator* (and especially if you make a living out of doing that), then you might care to cut out this column and pass it on to someone who is waiting to kill your ideas.

It might make him or her stop and think. It might hold up a mirror to show them how they sound. It might even pre-empt the excuses they are waiting to make.

THE 99 GREATEST IDEA KILLERS OF ALL TIME.
1. It doesn't grab me.
2. They'll never buy it.
3. We tried that before and it didn't work.
4. Doesn't fit the system.
5. Who's going to do it?
6. Let me run it by the C.F.K.I. (Committee for Killing Ideas).
7. I'll get back to you on this. This year.
8. Let me run it by my board/boss/subordinates/wife/my neighbour's cat. (Tick one.)
9. My people will talk to your people.
10. Great! Send me a memo.
11. Great! Why don't you c.c. me on your memo.
12. It's good, but Thais/Chinese/English/Malaysians/Japanese/etc./ are different from you or me.
13. It's been done to death.

14. The business office will bounce it.
15. It's not up to our standards.
16. Are we ready for this?
17. What will they say upstairs?
18. I like this idea. I have *always* liked this idea.
19. You can't argue with success.
20. The computer can't handle it.
21. It's not in our image.
22. It's not our style.
23. It sounds too simple.
24. It sounds too complicated.
25. It'll cost a fortune!
26. We'll never find the time to do it.
27. Will they understand it in Chiang Mai/Brisbane/Texas/Glasgow?
28. It's not us.
29. Let's talk.
30. The last guy who came up with that one isn't here anymore.
31. Don't fight City Hall.
32. Sounds crazy to me!
33. So, what else is new?
34. Just wait till they run the numbers.
35. We've never done anything like that.
36. Has anyone ever done anything like that before?
37. Didn't you know there's a recession going on?
38. Basically, I don't like it.
39. You gotta be kidding.
40. It turns me off.
41. It'll turn everybody off.
42. I hate it.
43. Ye-cch!
44. That creates as many problems as it solves.
45. (Laughter)
46. (Silence)
47. That's not your problem.
48. That's not your job.

49. That's not consistent with the way we do things here.
50. I've heard that one before.
51. Let's do lunch on this one.
52. Take a survey.
53. Let's meet on that some day.
54. It'll just cause problems.
55. How in the world did you come up with that?
56. They won't let you.
57. That's really off the wall!
58. Oh?
59. Oh...
60. Oh. I thought you were going to say something else.
61. Why don't you get your secretary to talk to my secretary.
62. Remember the client is pretty conservative (the customer is...the boss is..)
63. It'll hurt our dealers (our image...our backers...)
64. It's just not feasible.
65. Let's be realistic.
66. That's not my department.
67. The timing's not right.
68. Don't rock the boat.
69. Why don't you explain it in detail — on my answering machine.
70. Let's take the broad overview, the big picture.
71. Great idea — but not for us.
72. I have a better idea.
73. People will say we're silly.
74. People will say we're reckless.
75. What will people say?
76. Bring that up again next month.
77. It'll never sell.
78. It'll never work.
79. It'll never fly.
80. That would step on too many toes.
81. You'll offend 90% of your audience.
82. Let me play devil's advocate.
83. The women's libbers will kill you (or the FDA... or the trade press.)

84. Obviously, you misread the request.
85. Have you really given it much thought?
86. We need something more exciting.
87. Do you really think that would work?
88. Have you game-planned the worst-case scenario?
89. No one will know where you're coming from.
90. Now, that's a subject for another meeting.
91. Can I get back to you on this?
92. We'll lose our shirt.
93. That only solves half the problem.
94. Why bother?
95. Try again.
96. That's very provocative, but...
97. That's very interesting, but...
98. That's really fantastic, but...
99. Yes. But.

Now that I have given you 99 Idea Killers, watch how you use them. I recently sent a copy to one of my major clients, and he promptly turned the joke on me by sending me "10 GREAT EXCUSES". Some of them were pretty good.

But I'll be damned if I'll publish them here.

Get your own book, mate!

XV

The art of presentation (Part 1).

YES, BUT IT'S ONLY A 10×2 AD.

"Those who are going to be a business tomorrow are those who understand that the future, as always, belongs to the brave."

- William Bernbach
Doyle Dane Bernbach

MANY years ago from Australia, I phoned my Dad in New Delhi and said I had got a job in advertising. "Who will you advertise to," he said in wonderment, *"do they have a lot of Indians there?"*

Later, when I was able to make similar calls from London and New York, he had come to understand more about the business his son was into, but he never fully accepted it. And my telling him that advertising was the maximum amount of fun you could have with your clothes on, only made him more suspicious. After all, he never tired of telling me, he came from a family of businessmen, and "businessmen are people who have to work for a living."

Well, we do work, in advertising, and pretty hard at that.

We often sweat through inadequate briefs; capricious clients; foggy market readouts; itinerant team members forever preoccupied, it seems, with something else; self-perpetuating hierarchies; sudden international re-alignments; long hours and late nights.

And, more often than we care to admit, have it all fall down and fail when the client doesn't like it on the day we present.

Like any passionate relationship, we seem to hover between the twin obsessive fears of rejection, and that of being taken for granted.

To get over this, agencies sometimes go to extreme lengths on the Day of Presentation.

A hundred stories (many of them apocryphal) abound about ad agencies that took serious chances when selling themselves and their ideas to prospective clients. One English outfit, called Alan Brady Marsh, when pitching for the then six-million-pound British Rail account, kept chairman Lord Parker and his main executives hanging around for quite a while in a shabby waiting area. When the clients arrived, they were first ignored, and then a rather rude lady asked them if they wanted tea. She then served them in not-so-clean cups and got their milk and sugar orders all wrong. Finally, these British Rail executives, who had been treated considerably better in other agencies they had seen during their selection process that day, got fed up and stood up to leave. Suddenly, three heads popped up around the door frame (yes, you guessed correctly: they were the principals: Messrs. Alan, Brady and Marsh) speaking in unison: "Gentlemen, you have just experienced what the general travelling British public perceives to be the quality of service on British Rail. If you'd follow us now, please, to the boardroom where we will present you with advertising specifically designed to alter this perception."

Needless to say, they won the account.

An American agency, pitching for the Mercedes Trucks business, surprised the prospect by taking the visiting team in a long limo ride which ended at a Mercedes truck dealership, and then invited the clients-to-be to get in a Mercedes truck, the inside of which had been converted to become a conference room.

They, too, got the business.

But when does a presentation cross that fine line between hi-tech and hi-tacky?

Another Alan Brady Marsh story tells of that agency's pitch for the Honda (UK) business. Apparently, these gentlemen did their homework and were unable to learn anything about the Japanese client except that their boss liked British brass band music. The presentation went along as normal, fine creative work was presented and AB&M were unable to glean any reactions from the inscrutable client till they came down to street level to see him off. As they waited for the client's car, the group heard a fanfare and looked up and there, around the corner, marching in perfect formation, came the famous Coldstream Guards, playing the Honda jingle that had just been presented in the agency's offices a little while ago...

Seduced by all these stories, while working for an Australian agency, I once got carried away and, while presenting an idea based around how a product would "unchain" the housewife from the kitchen (it was a sort of hotplate on wheels), I opened my presentation by dumping 18 kilograms of iron anchor-chain on the client's beautiful mahogany table thereby scarring the table (and the client's psyche), probably for life. While it did manage to dramatise the unique selling proposition and focus everyone's attention on the matter at hand (which is what a good presentation should do), it also managed to get the agency almost fired from the business, and we retained it on condition that I would not be allowed to present my ideas directly to this client any more.

But they bought my idea!

Ever since then, I began to have an on-again off-again love affair with the idea of drama in presentations. I came to view them as a necessary evil, and I suppose my attitude reflected this at client meetings. After all, I liked to tell my colleagues, surely the substance of what we say must be more important than the style with which we say them.

Mustn't it?

In the second of this two part series on presentation skills, I will give you an answer that will totally amaze you. For this, I am forever indebted to Peter Rogen of Peter Rogen & Associates, of New York, whom my agency recently invited to speak to our people in this region.

Before I met Peter Rogen, my attitude was much more in tune with that of Sir Laurence Olivier. During the shooting for Marathon Man, filming was constantly delayed by Dustin Hoffman who, as an exponent of the Method School of Acting, caused many retakes as he constantly strove to put himself 'in character' so he could 'feel' his way into every scene. During one such delay, he decided to apologise to Sir Laurence who had, so far, been very patient and British about it all. "Hey, Larry, sorry about the delay, but ya know how it is, I have to get the method right, y'know?" Sir Laurence, to his credit, simply turned around and said with impeccable restraint, "Dear boy, why don't you try *acting* instead!"

Funny enough, the other people who have managed to change my opinion about the importance of good presentation are, believe it or not, bankers.

It has been my good fortune to create work for quite a few important banks. While creating advertising for all of Europe for Bank of America (the investment side of the business) and later some creative consultancy for Chase's initial forray into the Australian market as Chase AMP, I was astonished to discover how similar the banking business is to that of an advertising agency in structure of functions.

For instance, like us, they have people who deal with their clients (account executives), they have people who dream up new products and services (creative) and people who actually implement the policy. Not surprisingly bankers, too, strive to improve their presentation skills whenever they can. The difference, of course, is that they handle much bigger numbers with less drama, than you or I.

In the next chapter, I will try to deal with the question of style over substance. Style is important, but I can tell you right now that Alan Brady Marsh, the agency that won the British Rail advertising with their reception area theatrics, lost the business after a few campaigns.

You see, their presentation was OK, but their advertising perhaps just wasn't good enough.

So presentation will never be the final answer.

Thank goodness for *that.*

XVI

The art of presentation (Part 2).

YES, BUT IT'S ONLY A 10 X 2 AD.

"I couldn't hit a wall with a six-gun, but I can twirl one. It *looks* good."

- *John Wayne*

N the last chapter, I told you that I would share with you the answer to "what is more important: substance or style in a presentation?"

First, let me tell you that the answer you are about to read is not my answer. It is an answer by Peter Rogen, of Peter Rogen Associates of New York. He was in the region, recently, training people in various multinational organizations (including my own) on how to become better presenters.

But I was shocked that the question needed to be asked at all. The question was: which is more important in a presentation:

1. What you present, or

2. How you present, or

3. Who is doing the presentation?

So when Mr. Rogen asked us to allocate "percentages of importance" to the "What, How and Who", I did not hesitate to give a "50% importance" to the "What" section.

Mr. Rogen came right back and, striking out my 50%, wrote a big 7% against the "What" section. In other words, he meant, "How" something is said, and "Who" is seen to be saying it, is **90%** *of the entire ball game!* The "What" - or the substance - according to this distribution of weight, appeared to be incidental.

Now, even conceding that the research that was being used to support this argument was sourced by Peter Rogen and Associates, who directly benefit whenever companies such as ours buy into the importance of presentation techniques, it was still compelling enough to convince me to pay attention to his message. (It also served as a reminder to me that we live in an imperfect world!)

But the following is not just a summary of what Peter Rogen had to say. You can't condense a three-day course into two chapters. I urge you to get Mr. Rogen out here again. He used to be a Shakespearean actor who discovered that the hoi polloi of the corporate world were willing to pay him to introduce a bit of theatre to their boardrooms.

In New York, as in other parts of the world, the people who use him most are ad agencies (he was with Mr. Jocoby in the midst of a three-day course when the Saatchi buyout made the former Ted Bates' boss an instant squillionaire!) and banks (he can tell you all about Citibank world chief Walter Wriston's bedside reading habits!), and he believes deeply in audience participation rather than just dull lectures.

With a few hints from Peter, the following includes stuff I have learnt from my own

The prediction in this chapter about Mr. Bush's win was made seven months before the election. It earned Mr. Marwah a letter of thanks from the President (after he reminded the White House!)

presentations, good *and* bad: (in no particular order)

1. *Go in with the intention to communicate* - I have been to too many presentations where the intention was missing or, at least, not clearly projected. In a new business presentation, this intention should come through as a clear signal that you really want the business. Forget about the "of-course-they-know-we-want-their-business-or-else-why-do-they-think-we-are-going-through-this-pain?" syndrome. It's like opening and closing any sale. The best way to get an order still has to be: asking for it.

2. *Home work* - I don't know about bankers, but in advertising we often spend so much time trying to find out about the company we are pitching to that we forget about the *people* we are going to meet on the Big Day. A bit of intelligence, a bit of reconnaissance of the terrain never hurts. For instance, a friend of mine makes it a point to call the prospect before the presentation when he knows the guy is going to be absent. He then tries to obliquely find out as much as possible about the person from the secretary.

3. *Rehearsal* - I don't know a single great speaker or presenter who does not make a major effort to get to know the venue of the presentation and then rehearse *in situ,* as it were, the day before the pitch. Oh, I am sure they are there, it's just that I don't know them. Churchill used to work pretty hard on his speeches, and so did Lincoln. And so can you.

4. *Pitch it at the level of the decision maker* - Basically, that means that if you are pitching at some quiet, reserved sort of chap, dancing all over the room is probably going to scare him silly, and leave him with the impression that you are a great dancer. Which is great if you are selling dancing shoes, but sort of tragic if you're selling anything else.

5. *You can't bore people into buying from you* - Buying. Selling. That's what a presentation really is. In fact, an ad agency in Australia called The Campaign Palace starts *its letterhead* with the words: "Nobody buys much when they are asleep." While this remark is meant to apply to advertising, it applies just as well to presentations. I don't want to use this li'l ole chapter to alienate the guy who is obviously going to be the next leader of the free world (Hi, George! Remember you read it here first!) but one of the most pertinent remarks on the subject of presentation was made by George Bush to NBC's Linda Ellerbee in 1980 on the plane from Iowa to New Hampshire: "I'm not really as dull as you think I am." Remember, just saying it is not enough. This time around, Mr. Bush didn't go around just saying he wasn't a wimp. He demonstrated it by taking on Dan

Rather toe-to-toe on national television in a fiesty interview that made instant headlines around America.

So here is the moral about injecting interest in presentations:

If you've got it, flaunt it. And if you ain't got it, git some. And *then* flaunt it!

6. *Keep it focussed* - Peter Rogen could probably say this better than I can, but I'll try: "Tell 'em what you're about to say, then say it, and then sum up what you've just told them!" Simple though this may sound, we all run the risk of digressing forever into uncharted seas (and hence the risk of losing control of the presentation) when we start to wander away from the subject at hand. Even though, as Mick Jagger likes to say, "It's alright letting yourself go as long as you can get yourself back", a bit of digression is fine for the sake of interest and drama, but too much, and you might never return. And neither might the prospect's attention.

7. *Give them something to remember you by* - Ogilvy used to call it the mnemonic burr in advertising. In presentation, it can be a simple device that forever sears what you had to say in your presentation into the mind of the prospect. In New York, the Australian head of the Ted Bates operation once opened his report at a conference of Bates' chiefs on why he had been so successful with his new business meetings back home. "For a start," he said, "I don't use podiums like this one in my presentation room. In Sydney, when I took over, I hacked the rostrum we had to pieces with an axe. Like this!" Upon these words, Mr. Cousins is said to have taken out another axe in the Ted Bates boardroom in New York and split the rostrum he was using for his speech with a single blow! Ever since then, all the world heads who attended that conference remember this brash Australian and his message over everything else at the Bates conference.

My younger brother is the best presenter I know (I won't apologise for plugging my family so often - it is, after all, *my* book!) and he started in business with two rooms and three employees. But even in those days, everyone who came to see him would walk away with a wooden pencil inscribed, in golden letters, with the words **"I have just met Ranjan Marwah"**. I felt this was a tasteless exercise by a colossal ego (egos run rampant in our family) and I more or less said so. Now, he has come a long way from wooden pencils. He drives around in Rolls-Royces, but he still gives away pens to his special visitors. On a recent visit, I asked him why he doesn't inscribe them any more. "I don't need to," he said, "they know it's from me. Who else would give away a sterling silver pen, crafted by Tiffany's."

Who, indeed.

8. *Forget all the other rules you have just read if they stop you from winning* - To

114

use one of my favourite quotes from North Dallas Forty: "Your trouble is, you've never understood that seeing through the game is not the same as winning it."

And if you can't understand what that means, please don't worry about your presentation.

It'll be OK on the day. If OK is good enough for you.

For me, winning always feels better than OK. Winning feels *great.*

XVII

Cigarette advertising: The fire and the smoke.

"L'etat n'a pas a donner d'ordres eux entreprises. Sa tache est de creer le cadre propice aux initiatives individuelles."

— *Jacques Chirac, Prime Minister of France*

HELLO and Good Morning!

I thought we could start the day with a quote from the French this time, because they have a fairly good record with things like making the Statue of Liberty and inventing phrases like "liberte, egalite, fraternite" and so forth.

And all of these institutions come in handy when one is trying to talk sensibly and calmly about cigarette advertising these days. (Roughly translated, what the good minister from France was trying to say was that the state has no business ordering business around, but rather it should itself be in the business of trying to create a favorable and fair environment for individual initiatives.)

Another reason for starting the day with a French flavor is: I have recently given up smoking cigarettes — in order to qualify for writing this chapter! — and the method I used, a French lady friend just told me, was the De Gaulle method.

Apparently, De Gaulle gave up cigarettes at the toughest moment of his life. There he was, somewhere in the south of England, chafing at the bit and waiting to reclaim his country from the Germans and boom! He stopped smoking. Just like that! Many years later, a reporter asked him how he did it. "It was simple really," said the general. "I got up one morning and *told my wife and two aides-de-camp that I had stopped."* The reporter went away scratching his head till somebody explained to him that Mon Generale was a man of such high self-esteem that, once he had told the people nearest to him that he was going to stop, his pride would not let him slide back!

Well, the general I ain't. And I am going through hell. And my self-esteem suffers terribly when I slide and cheat and take a drag of somebody's cigarette. I also endanger my health and go around feeling like a drug addict.

And since I have been smoking 30 cigarettes a day for over 20 years, I now begin to realize that I *have* been a drug addict. And the drug has been nicotine. And I now know exactly what withdrawal means.

Already, I have managed to have a few pointless arguments with my friends. My secretary, my maid, my driver (isn't it great — living in the East!) and two of my clients have already strongly hinted that I would be a much more tolerable person if I started smoking immediately.

Should this object, this pinch of processed leaves wrapped in paper, be allowed to continue to cause such havoc.

Should we ban its advertising in the few countries where it is still permitted?

As I go through the torture of quitting even as I write these words, my answer has to be: "No."

Because, as long as I can buy cigarettes in the open market, legally, I can't for the life of me understand why I can't be allowed to advertise them, on any medium I choose. For governments around the world to ban cigarettes from TV screens and the like, while agreeing to take billions in tobacco taxes, has to be the most incomprehensible bit of double dealing since the invention of the wooden nickel.

Too much of anything is bad for you. We all know that. When I was a child, I was constantly reminded that too much sex (if I ever got that fortunate) would make me blind. But my clarity of vision today is more a happy accident of fate than a tribute to my powers of restraint. Cigarettes, of course, are addictive. Like a glass of beer or wine, after a hard day, a cigarette will act like a relaxing sedative. But if you drink a bottle or two of rotgut just to get legless every night, the chances are it will do your liver a modicum of harm.

In fact, the pollution caused by cigarettes would have to increase before it could begin to seriously compete with the pollution levels from traffic smoke in so many cities today.

But the real issue here is how much of a policing role a government should play in people's lives. If we can legally endorse a product as fit for sale, but declare it unfit for advertising, where would it stop? Would we, for instance, give permission for advertising fish and poultry in greater proportion to red meat, or reduce salt advertising, or ban cooking oils every time there is a scare from the health-fad-of-the-day?

Nowadays, cigarette advertising has little impact on overall sales. Wherever cigarette advertising has been banned, it has not affected the trends in sale, before and after the ban. In other words, if the trend was down, it stayed that way. And if it was up, it kept going up.

Cigarette advertising does not affect trends because it is not aimed at non-smokers, these days. It is aimed at brand switching, which I would have thought should be a market's birthright in any free economy.

The primary cause of people starting smoking is, believe it or not, peer group pressure, not advertising. Or the environment: for instance, parents who smoke. Which means we are now legislating to make up for the sins of omission of our parents.

Cigarette smoking among women is going up, and yet there is very little cigarette advertising aimed at women. Cigarette advertising is banned in the Eastern Bloc countries, and yet cigarette smoking has been going up consistently in those countries.

I gave up cigarettes. But before I did, I switched to low-tar cigarettes. And how do you think I found out about those low-tar cigarettes. And how do you think I found out about those *low-nicotine* low-tar beauties? Through their advertising.

120

Right now, I feel sick from the pain of quitting cigarettes. But it makes me sicker to think that we can sit back and allow Big Brother into our lives through the back door. The thin end of the wedge is when Somebody Up There can legislate and tell us what is, and what is not, good for us. If it is cigarettes today (okay to sell, but not okay to advertise), it could be whatever is unfashionable tomorrow.

And before you tell me that I have a vested interest, let me tell you that, as I write this, the company I work for does not advertise cigarettes. And I have never met anyone from The Tobacco Institute in my life.

But would I advertise cigarettes if the chance came along tomorrow? Why not? Cigarette advertising, like anti-smoking advertising, should be left to the personal beliefs of the people involved in the enterprise. Just like political advertising for one or another party.

You can't legislate personal beliefs.

Because you cannot, and should not, legislate the way people think.

I started this article with a quote from France, so let me end with a quote from David Tench, legal advisor to the U.K.'s Consumers' Association, from his speech to the Law Society in Paris in 1983:

> **There is only one thing worse than misleading advertising — and that is no advertising at all.**

Cigarette, anyone?

XVIII

Writing for radio (Part 1).

HOW NOT TO WRITE
A RADIO SPOT.

"The Martians have landed. But please don't panic."

- *Orson Welles*

IT was a hoax, but as a broadcast, live on radio, it set fire to the imagination of thousands of people. As the young Orson Welles spoke (see quote opposite) with convincing sound effects for hours "live" from the spot in New Jersey "where the flying saucer has landed," people streamed either to, or away from, the imaginary landing site.

Roads clogged. Houses were left open. Bedlam prevailed.

I don't know how many decades ago it was, that night when young Orson seared his name into radio history with his "invasion from outer space," but that was the night, more than anything else, that marks the moment when the raw, untrammeled power of the medium was unleashed in a manner that was recognized by all. Radio was king.

And then a funny thing happened to radio.

A funny thing called television.

While I would not, for a minute, dispute the power of television, the spot that radio now occupies in people's minds is disproportionately smaller than its true potential.

And because people don't approach it with the respect it deserves, the writing for radio that we hear these days is often abysmal. It uses only a tenth of the power of the medium. And if you are the one paying for radio advertising from your pocket, 90% could often be going to waste purely because of the unimaginative scripts that are used to create the ads in the first place.

1. — *FSFX:* In radiospeak sfx means "sound effects." In Marwahspeak (my own invention for radio writers!) FSFX stands for Fear of Sound Effects. Many experts at writing for print sit petrified in front of a page marked "radio copy" simply because they don't know how to use the silences and the sound effects. And yet radio is the one medium where a few sounds can make a cheap production sound like a million dollars.

The Radio Marketing Bureau in the United States often puts out fantastic promotional material (on radio, naturally) that sells the medium at its true potential. Here, from memory, is a radio ad that they distributed about the potential of radio:

Male Voice (Announcer): Here we are gathered at Lake Michigan with thousands of people waiting to see a great event. We are about to see a great event. We are about to drain Lake Michigan, fill it up with whipped cream and put a giant Marachino cherry at the top. And we'll do this *right before your eyes!*

(sfx: Huge draining noise begins) And here we go! All the water in Lake Michigan being drained away before your very eyes and now, the whipped cream (sfx: thump thump of large machines being turned on). The swirls of cream — *look at* all

that cream — begin to fill up the largest lake of all *(sfx:* glug glug of cream, and whoosh whoosh as it sounds like it is filling up the last little bit of the lake, *sfx:* oohs and aahs of crowd plus excited whispering of someone who is obviously standing near the announcer at this big event right at the edge of Lake Michigan) — and now, ready or not, the giant 25-ton Marachino cherry *(sfx:* ever increasing sounds of rotor blades, aahs and oohs of crowd) — yes, you can see the helicopter and look, dangling below, that GIANT Marachino cherry, and oh goodness! *Look!* they're going to let go! — *(sfx:* whistling sound as cherry drops on lake) — here it comes, faaaalling through the air!! (sfx: BIG PLOP) and they've done it! (sfx: crowd noises, excited whispers) a giant lake, filled with whipped cream, right before your eyes, topped with a 25-ton cherry.''

Try doing that on television.

And of course, when you heard this commercial, you *saw* it as well. Which brings me to my second point:

2. — *Radio is nothing but painting pictures in your mind:* Go find someone really dumb. (You know, lights are on but no one's home.) Find an empty mind, if you like, and try some word pictures on this person. You'll find that any mind, no matter how limited, can get the message if you let it draw its own pictures. All you have to do is supply the words and sound effects.

In fact, sometimes you don't even have to have the sound effects. Just imagination will do. (And when you commission a radio ad, imagination is what you are really paying for.) Radio can go deeper into the listener's mind because it can, when done properly, demand and get 100% listener involvement.

Here is an ad for Guinness from London. All you need to know is that the ad line for Guinness currently in the U.K. is "Guinness. Pure Genius." You're going to hear a man talking about a dog. Now try and figure out what the dog is doing (and how much it would cost you to do this on television!): And this ad is not from decades ago. It ran last year in London.

March, 88: Radio Script. Guinness. 60 seconds.

Male Narrator Voice: "The tall blond man dressed in black didn't seem the least bit disappointed when his dog came last in the obedience competition. He merely shrugged his shoulders and drank some more Guinness. Later, in the car, the tall blond man talked to his dog, as all of us do."

Man with American Accent: "You're a smart dog, but sometimes you're just too smart. You could have won the trophy with your eyes closed. You know it. I know it. You just had to sit there, roll over and go fetch the right hanky. Easy stuff. But you just sat there looking down your nose at the whole thing. You want to tell me why?"

Narrator: "The dog, needless to say, said nothing. He merely put the car in second gear and turned past the sign that said 'Pure Genius'."

Man with American Accent: "Now you may be wondering why the dog was driving the car. Reason is, I never drink and drive."

That's radio. Pure radio.

As you can see, there are some obvious difficulties in writing about radio. But writing for radio should be no problem if you learn to love the medium.

I wish this page was an audio cassette so I could try to demonstrate for you the true magic of the medium to help you look at it through reawakened eyes. In the next chapter, in the second part of this two-part series on radio, I plan to devote most of the space to some radio scripts that I like and to let your mind draw its own pictures.

3. — *Hearing a script is not good enough:* But before I close today, let me leave you with ONE good rule of thumb to help you judge a good radio ad: if all you do *hear* is what the writer is trying to say, dump it. But if you can *see* a picture, if the script can *take* you there, buy it. You've got gold.

4. — *"Who listens to radio?"* was the title of another U.S. Radio Marketing Bureau campaign in the early sixties, when they first seriously decided to defend their turf against television. They commissioned Stan Freeberg and Leslie Uggams who came with a song that went something like:

> **"Who listens to radio?**
> **Who listens to radio?**
> **It's with you every night, in the long traffic fight,**
> **And in the morning with your toast and marmaladio!**
> **It's the go-anywhere-medium they call radio!**
> **Who listens to radio?**
> **Just ten million six hundred thousand people that's all!"**

Some people say that radio is "aural wall paper." But they are also the people who write boring scripts for radio.

In my opinion, they are also *themselves* usually unprofessional people.
Mediocre people. Boring people.

XIX
Writing for radio (Part 2).

HAVEN'T YOU HEARD
OF COCONUT SHELLS?

RECORDING

"If you're going to play the game properly, you'd better know every rule."

- *Barbara Jordan*

can't think of any rules for radio advertising other than the ones that apply to advertising in general (or other than the ones I tried to list in the last chapter).

You've got to be intrusive, entertaining, involving, telegraphic, persuasive, dramatic, memorable and relevant like any other kind of advertising.

Except radio is more fun.

Soon after I got my first job in Sydney many years ago, a rather fat copywriter friend of mine called Jonathan Coleman (who the children of my Australian readers will recognize as the chap who later twisted and warped the minds of an entire generation as star host of Simon Townsend's Wonder World!) and I decided that we would have a crack at writing funny stuff for radio in The Lucky Country.

For me, that first bit of on-air material on 2JJ (now 2JJJ) started a love affair with this medium that grew passionate with time. Daytime, I worked in advertising — and night and weekends, I took what opportunity I could find to work on radio comedy or, later, television programs of any sort.

For Jonathan it eventually spelt a goodbye to advertising. Today, his adult contemporary music show ('Cover-to-Cover' affiliated with the U.S.' Westwood One) goes through the MCM network to 20 stations across Australia, sponsored by Diet Coke. And his TV show ('Saturday Morning Live') also plays live across Australia and PNG.

Since I promised to bring you more radio scripts in this chapter, I asked Jonathan to help me select them. Here is our choice.

Try to hear these commercials instead of just reading them, please. (Read the bits where it says sfx — sound effects — and try to imagine the sounds):

1. *How do you use silence?* Here is an example of silence being used to devastating effect by Black & Decker.

Black & Decker 'Makes smoke make a noise'

MVO: You are asleep in your bed at night. A fire has broken out downstairs. This is the sound the smoke makes as it creeps upstairs to suffocate you...

(Five seconds silence) ... and this is the sound the same smoke makes when you have a Black & Decker Smoke Alarm...

SFX: Smoke Alarm Bleeping

...The Black & Decker Smoke Alarm. It makes smoke make a noise. And it's only Pounds 9.99 from all London branches of Woolworths.

2. *How do you demonstrate a product benefit?* Here is the late Leonard Rossiter helping you to see the IBM typewriter in your head:

IBM Tripewriter

LEONARD ROSSITER: Watch your secretary as she uses her tripewriter. Every time ... what? Ah! Typewriter. Yes. Every time she bakes a miscake, she goes... makes a mistake ... she goes black and starts ... goes back and types it a pain ... again.

Now if you were to get her an IBM 82C, no matter how hairless she might be...er careless, she'd hardly be hairless, would she? Well, she could be I suppose ... need a wig... hrmph ... all she has to do is dress a few muttons and bombs ... press a few buttons ... got it! and bombs her ankle ... her uncle ... Bob's her uncle. Yes, he's definitely her uncle.

Effortless collections ... I'll correct that, sorry ... corrections ... effortless corrections. So visit IBM in Pigmore Street and ask ... must be Wigmore ... and ask to see (deep breath) the IBM 82C Correcting Golf Ball Typewriter ... Ha Ha ... got that white ... er ... right! Oh, what a pity this scrit wasn't ... what a scritty this pipt ... what a pity this script wasn't triped on one.

3. *How to use a current event to sell your product?* Remember Camp David? I remember laughing when I woke up to this Aussie commercial for Eggline during the peace talks in America.

Eggline

SFX: Phone ring, pick up.
Anwar: Menachem, it's Anwar!
Menachem: Hello ... Anwar, ha ha ... Anwar ... er Anwar who?
Anwar: Remember me. From Egypt. We live next door.

132

Menachem: **Oh! That six-day Anwar. Ha ha. Yes ... oh ... what can I do for you, my friend?**

Anwar: **Just a small favour, Menachem...**

Menachem: **Name it and it's yours ... anything!**

Except the West Bank ... the Gaza Strip ... all the oil wells.

Anwar: **Manny, I was just looking for a new recipe, a few of my neighbours are dropping in tonight and I wanted to ...**

Menachem: **A recipe? Say no more. Do I have a recipe for you. Ha ha ha!**

Anwar: **Do you?**

Menachem: **Scrumptious, from the Eggline I got it!**

Anwar: **The what?**

Menachem: **The Eggline! Eggline! 20999 Sydney! You just call them and they give you delicious egg recipes every week, free hm! Hm! First of all you b... eh! Who are the neighbours you are entertaining, Anwar?**

Anwar: **Uh ... Saudi Arabia and Libya (Pause) Hello? (Pause). Shalom, Manny, can you hear me now?**

Operator: **Believe me. The line is dead!**

4. *How to tap into a nation's pride?* MoJo-MDA (Mo stands for Alan Morris and Jo stands for Alan Johnston) have kept alive a refreshing jingle for Toohey's beer that almost everyone of 16 million Australians can now sing at the drop of a keg. Here is the long-distance phone call that leads into the jingle and makes you want to reach for a tinnie, instantly:

CROOK BEER

MVO: Hullo Dad ... Dad, it's me...oh, you got my letter from London... oh, the beer's crook, Dad ... got me card from Calcutta, Dad ... Calcutta, the beer's crook, Dad ... Bali, not bad ... America, people couldn't have been nicer ... but the beer ... Brazil beauty ... I was just in time for the carnival ... couldn't drink the beer though... Dad, the reason I'm ringing is well, I just got off the plane, Dad ... I'm home ... how do you reckon I feel ... (music up)

Chorus Jingle: ("I feel like a Tooheys or two!") (repeat)

MVO: Three weeks without a Toohey's ... a man could die of thirst.

5. *Another demonstration:* "Look! It's thicker!" Can you show the thickness of cooking foil on radio? Can you ever!

THICK

ANNCR: "We decided to ask three different cooking foils a simple question. First, a cheap, thin brand. Tell me, what's 2 and 2?"

CHEAP, THIN BRAND: "4."

ANNCR: "Very good."

"Then we ask an ordinary, middleweight foil."

(He gives a little cough.)

"What's 2 and 2?"

MIDDLEWEIGHT FOIL. "Very easy."

ANNCR: "Please. Then we asked Comalco Alfoil."

"Comalco Alfoil, what's 2 and 2?"

COMALCO ALFOIL: "Uh, dah. Aw, gee. Ah. Dat's a hard one."

ANNCR: "There you are. Positive proof that Comalco Alfoil is very thick. And when you're a foil, it's smart to be thick."

The importance of radio was brought home to me quite dramatically in a chance encounter in America last year.

Last year, I was taken sick during a New York summer with a cold and I rushed out from the casting session to buy a sweater. And where should I walk into but Barney's. So there I am, buying this woolly from this young punk who is dying to go to lunch and suddenly this old man arrives. The old man is talking his head off and the salesman sneers and tells me: "This is old Mr. Barney, up from his retirement in Florida because he just can't leave us in New York, alone!" I am electrified. I started talking to this old guy and he says: "Why did you come to Barney's?" and I say: "I love your advertising from all the award annuals I used to read in Australia!" This made his eyes sparkle and we talked for an hour about his ads and his business.

Then, he says something that amazes me. He confesses that radio advertising was something that had helped him more in establishing his business than anything else he could think of. Really, I say to him, explain. He does! "When I started with my first small shop, as a tailor, I wanted to advertise but I could not afford it. A radio salesman offered me some ads at a discount. Well, that summer, I bought more radio ads than I could afford, and even though I was a very small shop, people thought I was big, and that is how I became so big!"

Today, his sons are about to expand — really take his chain into the big leagues. But I don't think there are too many Madison Avenue people who know that story of how it all began.

6. *Getting to the public for social good.* When working for Lintas:Sydney, I was asked by the State Government to devise a campaign to discourage people from drinking to the point of blood alcohol level above .05% before driving. Rather than get clever and funny, I asked a mother whose family had suffered the trauma of crashing into a drunk driver. I asked her to speak into the mike, on camera, with her own words. This is part of a campaign that won radio awards around the world. But my greatest award was when the Transport Ministry told us that we had helped to reduce the road toll by over 30% that holiday season. Here is what she said. All I helped do was edit it down to 60 seconds and used it as is:

Traffic Authority of NSW
Random Breath Testing

RUTH

ANNCR: One day in Sydney, Ruth was in a car hit by a drunk driver.

RUTH: We were about 5 minutes from home. The fear that Bob and the twins were going to die ... and there was blood and glass absolutely everywhere and police and ambulances and fire brigades. It was unbelievable. I was in the back and I was kneeling on the seat and I was holding Simone's head, that was one of the twins, with one hand and I was holding Bob's with the other (sobs, starts crying), because the bottom half of his face had come away and all I kept thinking was if I held it they might be able to put it together ... and it wasn't until the next morning it hit me, just how bad things were, I don't know what he could do but I am sure he must feel devastated that somebody virtually took over his life.

ANNCR: Stay under .05 or get off the road.

These days, *anyone* can learn to create with sound. All you have to do is decide you want to *speak* your next letter to someone overseas. Just take a reel-to-reel tape-recorder or an ordinary recorder around, and build a library of sounds — your home, your office, your factory, your street. Anything. Record a few words. Your ideas on anything. Pick a subject and try to paint a picture in the mind of the person you are writing to. Try putting the whole thing on audiocassette and send it off.

The response you get will be, I promise, totally different to the last letter you wrote to the same person.

XX

The great outdoors: The fastest medium of them all (Part 1).

Heineken refreshes the parts other beers cannot reach.

Heineken - The line you are looking at is one that this beer manufacturer has been using for over ten years. This poster appeared at a time when JR, the character played by Larry Hagman in Dallas, was synonymous with all that is dirty, low down, double dealing and yucky when it comes to winning corporate or family battles. This campaign made this beer the #1 imported beer in the UK.

The Met - Take the tube instead of taking your car. If you ever needed a better reason to leave your car at home and take the State Transport, maybe a real parking ticket flapping in the breeze as you drive by will help you!

THIS is my first election year in an Asian country since I got into the advertising business. I wonder if they will have political ads.

Imagine a picture of a long queue of unemployed people waiting to get paid their unemployment benefits outside an English dole office.

And below this picture, imagine a simple statement:

Labour Isn't Working. Vote Conservative.

With stunning statements such as this one on a huge outdoor 48-sheet poster, the Saatchi boys helped to win for Margaret Thatcher an election result that started Britain on the road to recovery and a magnificent eight years which has revived the economy, strengthened the pound and allowed that embattled rocky isle off the northern coast of France to walk tall in the world of geopolitics.

Now I am not suggesting that one outdoor poster won the election for Maggie Thatcher. I am saying that there was a time Tim Bell of Saatchi's had more access to her than some of the junior ministers of her cabinet, and it wasn't because of his good looks. Sure, the Conservatives had a good product in the first place, but great advertising didn't hurt.

Over the next two chapters, I will try to share with you my views on outdoor advertising: Some do's and don'ts.

But to help you get the feel of the medium right away, let's try a little exercise together. Imagine you are at the top of a very tall building. Imagine you have a very, very large piece of paper in your hand and a giant marker.

Now look down. (Don't worry about your vertigo, it's only an exercise!) Do you see that long line of cars down there? Ok. Now focus on the red car, ten cars down the line. See it? Right. Now all you have to do is attract the attention of the driver.

Assuming he is not caught in a traffic jam, you are going to have to hurry, because look, there he goes!

C'mon, quick, say something. Anything. Oh, it has to be tasteful, so he won't turn off. Telegraphic because he can't spare more than a glance (oops! he almost had an accident!). Witty and memorable because you want him to remember what you say. And relevant because, having got his attention, you wouldn't want to sell him hot air.

Ready? Go.

Not fair, huh? OK. Take a whole day to think about it. In fact, take a month. Get an artist, photographers, smart copywriters. Forget the paper and giant magic marker. Get some spotlights and hire the entire side of the building.

Bluegrass Jeans - *Only in Australia! Well, if this ad needs explaining about what it is that makes it just right for its target audience, maybe we ought to turn to the next poster.*

Drink like a fish. Eat like a pig. Smell like a rose.

Ombo Breath Freshener - *The nicest thing about Poster Advertising is, you don't need to explain it. All I can say about this one is: It is also quintessentially Australian. Plain speaking, direct, aimed at an area roughly between the eyes!*

You are beginning to get the picture about outdoor hoardings. It is called a 50 miles-per-hour medium because, even though the hoarding or poster site is static, people pass by it at amazing speeds (barring, as I said, traffic jams!).

You are also beginning to get an idea of what I shall be writing about for the next two chapters.

For starters, in this chapter are four outdoor posters that I rather like, and ones that serve to illustrate some important points about writing for The Great Outdoors: The Fastest Medium of them all. Keep in mind, please, as you study these four examples, that the message has to be short and snappy (someone once said that eight words is too much) to be seen at all. And if it is not interesting (like any advertising) no one's going to read it OR REMEMBER IT.

Well, if you are interested in outdoor advertising, this should get you going.

Remember, some of the best creatives in the world prefer to *start* writing a campaign for this medium even if the client is not going to use the medium! The reason, they say, is that nothing focuses the mind on a problem as having to write for the Great Outdoors: You have to come up with a great idea, the words have to work with the pictures to complete the sentence, and you haven't got the time to fool around. *You are just not given enough time.*

Think about it.

Isn't life a bit like that?

XXI

The great outdoors: The fastest medium of them all (Part 2).

AHH! THE GREAT OUTDOORS.

NO NICKERS is actually the name of panties made by Holeproof in Australia. The reason these panties are called NO NICKERS by the manufacturer is that once you have them on, they fit you so perfectly that you don't see the 'nicker line' and your dress fits smoothly over it. What better ad for this promise than to have a beautiful 3-D derriere protruding with this amazing line. Naturally, you are going to wait for the wind to blow. And when it does...

NO NICKERS
...voila, you see the nickers! And you realise that their promise was true. You never knew, did you? Was she or wasn't she? That's the idea.

MI-FANCY
Here's another way to bring the product promise to life on location: Mi-Fancy Bird Seed actually sprinkled their product on the poster site in large quantities. The result? The site was always full of birds in living demonstration of the claim.

THE last chapter raises an interesting question: What is 'outdoors'? Just those large posters we pass by on the roads?

The answer (according to me, anyway) is: Outdoors is anything that isn't indoors! And what do I mean by this? Allow me to elaborate on this shaft of wisdom.

I would call posters on the London Underground outdoors. I would call the jackets on live cows that an enterprising farmer rented for advertisers' messages on London train commuter routes, outdoors. I would call that memorable Wembley final (in the days before the Cup went to unlikely teams like Wimbledon, for goodness sake!), when a sign near the goalpost said, "Happy Birthday, Harry", outdoors. (Incidentally, when the dozens of people called the TV stations trying to find out if they were the "Harry" in question, a poster company finally admitted that it had created this message to dramatise the power of the medium!) I would call that big KOMATSU mega-tractor that sits solemnly atop a downtown Tokyo building, outdoors. I would call those dirigibles that Alan Bond makes that sell Fuji and British Caledonian, outdoors, as I would the Goodyear blimp that has enlivened many a Superbowl. Skywriting is outdoors. I'd even call those spray-printing techniques that a friend of mine is importing into Hong Kong to write ad messages on eggs, outdoors (because you can buy the eggs at outdoor markets and then *carry* them indoors!).

But the heart of the medium, limited only by our imagination, is still those magnificent posters that, in color and black and white and three dimensional cutouts, sometimes make my heart miss a beat when I see them on the highways of the world.

In the middle of that fuel crisis of long ago, my mind still crowds with the images created by people like Si Liam, the DDB New York Impressario of Outdoors, and his team who gave us messages like a cartoon drawing of a petrol bowser being pointed by a man at his own head with the headline: OR GET A VOLKSWAGEN. Or a large tumbler which, at first glance, looked like it had a couple of fizzy Alka Seltzers going in and closer examination revealed a VW Logo on the bubbling tablets. The headline? "IF GAS PAINS PERSIST."

With this chapter are some more of my favorites:

ARALDITE

And how about the famous car stuck on the poster to advertise a glue. They created a furor with this ad, and followed it up with two cars, one on top of another. The last poster in this series had the same poster-site with a gaping hole in it, and NO cars! The headline was: "AND HOW DID THEY GET IT OFF?" A magnificent tribute to the adhesive powers of ARALDITE.

JOHNNY WALKER BLACK

If your train is about to go into a tunnel on the London Underground, why not take advantage of it with a good ad? Johnny Walker Black did. With wit and humour and style.

XXII

The great outdoors: The fastest medium of them all (Part 3).

OUTDOOR CAN REALLY GRAB
THE CONSUMER'S ATTENTION.

"On the 2nd of September, I will take off my top," promised this lady, and all of Paris was a buzz and agog! Will she? Won't she?

She did. You are beginning to get the idea. Now all of Paris was saying: "Hey, she is promising to take off the bottom on the 4th. Will she, won't she?"

On the 4th of September, she did! But she turned around. And the headline now said: "Avenir, the poster company that keeps its promises." Brilliant, non?

AS you can see, I have devoted the concluding part of this series on the Great Outdoors to the posters themselves. Showing you the great outdoor posters, surely, makes more sense than my waffling on about them endlessly.

As you watch the Silk Cut campaign, remember this: Even now there are people in London going around saying *"the consumer will never understand the wit"* and *"Oh, they've gone too far this time!"* and stuff like that. But they are all advertising people. The consumer, in fact, not only understood, but thronged to buy Silk Cut in large numbers.

In a market where the laws forbid you from saying almost anything about cigarettes, except the health warning, here is a campaign that is just about singlehandedly responsible for the following quote from the Feb 19, 1988, issue of *Campaign* (the British advertising trade paper): "In a relatively short time, Silk Cut has moved from the country's fifth most popular cigarette brand to second by value behind Benson and Hedges. It is the best selling low tar cigarette with 50% of the market."

Not bad, huh?

LOW TAR As defined by H.M. Government DANGER: Government Health WARNING: CIGARETTES CAN SERIOUSLY DAMAGE YOUR HEALTH.

LOW TAR As defined by H.M. Government
Warning: MORE THAN 30,000 PEOPLE DIE EACH YEAR IN THE UK FROM LUNG CANCER
Health Departments' Chief Medical Officers

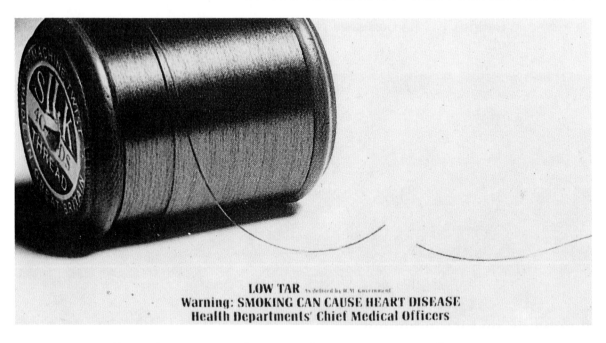

LOW TAR As defined by H.M. Government
Warning: SMOKING CAN CAUSE HEART DISEASE
Health Departments' Chief Medical Officers

Silk Cut. From #5 to #2 by treating the consumer as an intelligent being.

XXIII

Encourage your ad agency to make a mistake.

AND NOW I'D LIKE TO
PRESENT THE
MEDIA, FATSO.

"We are in the growth business. We happen to sell toys."

- *Mr. Lazarus, CEO of booming Toys "R" US in a 1988 interview with Fortune magazine."*

NOW, how tough is the title of this chapter to swallow with your morning coffee?

After all, you're thinking, what is this guy asking me to do? Rush in to work next week and tell my agency to trash their best campaign and go lay an egg?

Not really. My thinking goes something like this:

First, ask yourself what your business really is.

No, I don't mean the manufacturing or servicing of widgets. Your factory or your people do that. I mean, your business. What do you *do,* every day?

I'll tell you. You make decisions every day. *That's* the business you are in. Personally. You.

So now, how many of these decisions of yours are correct and sound and income-enhancing? How many times do you bomb when the bottom line is in the balance, the inventory is on hold, the R&D people are screaming for more money, the sales manager wants to hire or fire people or when you're about to ink a new distribution deal. Well, if you're able to examine your soul half as clearly as your face when you're shaving (or putting on make-up, ma'am), you might come up with a figure of at least 10 to 20 percent. These are times when, in retrospect, you know you were wrong. (Don't worry, nobody's found you out yet!)

In fact, I remember in the early '80's when an American-trained manager came back to Britain to run an ailing business and was later interviewed about the one single factor that, in his opinion, led to an almost three-fold increase in his company's turnover in less than five years. *"It would have been the ability to accept the inevitability of mistakes being made,"* he said, *"when one is in the midst of steering a company to new directions and higher goals."* He explained how he had called a meeting, in his first year, of all his main business chiefs and told them that the fact that they were all on salaries did not mean that they were not also business people. He told them that he expected each of them to be truly entrepreneurial the following year and that he wanted them to make at least 25% incorrect decisions before their next annual get-together!

Imagine that. 1 out of 4 decisions. Deliberately wrong!

This chief executive officer was phenomenally successful because he freed up his managers, his income-generators, to trust their own judgment rather than waiting on head office to constantly hold their hands. And red ink turned to black in less than 16 months to the tune of millions of pounds.

155

Now, the chances are that you, too, probably have a head office to report to. If you find that frustrating and painful and needless sometimes, must you inflict the same plague on your own people?

But I am not here to tell you how to run your business. I simply happen to believe that your advertising agency is the one area most in need of independent decision-making. And stifling their initiative only means you are shortchanging yourself.

The key people in your ad agency are like your business managers. But they have a tougher job.

Because they deal in an endeavor that almost everyone approaches with their mouth open. Everybody has an opinion about every ad — which is odd, considering that no one can tell you except in hindsight what is really good or bad about an ad campaign.

And an ad agency that lives in terror of what your multi-tiers of management might think of their latest campaign — an agency that must, for its survival, try to respond in advance (before it even sits down to create the campaign) to what your opinion might be — is bound to create safe advertising.

And safe advertising is dull advertising. Boring advertising.

And boring advertising sends people to sleep.

And the consumer doesn't buy much when he/she is asleep.

If you want your agency to create advertising that is noticed, advertising that stands out from the crowd, then join your agency in a partnership of hearts and minds and accept that you are both to some extent venturing forth into uncharted seas.

Is that terribly different from any other entrepreneurial decision you make everyday?

Safe advertising, because it doesn't get noticed, is probably the most dangerous advertising of all.

Dangerous, because you are in the danger of wasting your money as the ad dies — unnoticed and unsung and unheard.

With each ad that I create, I like to think that I join with my client in a major enterprize.

If the venture pays off — and with the tools of research and personal judgment and a dozen other lamp posts to guide our way, it often does — the rewards can be incalculable. But a journey like that cannot be undertaken in an atmosphere of mistrust and a master-servant relationship. Because then the imperative becomes not what both

156

parties stand to gain, but where they could both fall, and lose.

An enterprize that drapes itself in the oppressive mists of fear is doomed before it begins.

Especially an enterprize like the creation of noticeable, dramatic, entertaining, original, telegraphic, relevant and persuasive advertising.

In our business, in advertising, we look failure straight in the eye every day of our lives and we press on, regardless. For no man ever scaled the heights without occasionally looking down to conquer, along the way, his fears of falling.

So, come Monday, loosen up a little.

Tell your ad agency to go on and make a mistake.

It could become the best business decision you make this year.

XXIV

Putting our own house in order.

"**"If you don't buy this ad, I will jump out of the window."**"

- George Lois to reluctant client in Manhattan skyscraper office."

SOMETHING funny happened to advertising on the way back from the theater: We lost some of our drama and impact.

We lost some of the urgency, some of the pizzaz, some of our persuasion. Some agencies with their layers of hierarchies and departments stand in danger of losing their reason for being: advertising!

The your-people-will-talk-to-my-people syndrome took over as research shifted from being friend and guide to dictator. Risk, the heart of many great advertisements, took a back seat while "corporate responsibility" took over the steering wheel.

In the midst of this, an international chief made the following speech at the world conference of his agency heads, and implored them to involve the creative people more in the decision-making process and the client contact areas.

In less than a year, that agency jumped from #8 to #6 internationally, and today stands poised for breaking into the top five.

He encouraged discussion within each branch agency, and threw open the doors of debate so that people could unashamedly strive for excellence. Here is what he said to his international gathering of Chief Executives and Creative Directors:

"I think the demands that we must meet in today's competitive environment require a seemless management team. Sharing the management of clients, and the management of the creative process, as a single business purpose.

And in this environment, these debates should leave people feeling satisfied, that the purpose of creative excellence was served, not whether they won or lost.

And in this environment everyone should be striving to make the work better, because they know we do.

In fact, in this environment, our attitude about how much better the work can be, and our attitude about putting the work before politics, will be the attitude to emulate, our people won't aspire any higher than we do, or work harder.

161

Then there's one more trick to it, we must not attempt to do it individually.

I particularly address this to those of you who are agency heads, and those of you who are creative directors.

If you attempt to do it individually, you'll each be only half effective, or worse, doing it individually means the agency will only be half committed, or at diverse purposes. The by-product will be internal politics and factions and the purpose we're here to serve will get under-delivered and undermined.

To really turn on the heat, it takes a dedicated team of two. The agency's management must be a union of both essential parts: creative management, as well as general management.

Do you always have to agree? Of course not. But you always have to agree that it's OK to disagree. And that you should establish which one of you is to have the last word on what copy gets recommended to the client, should it come to that, and you both must get behind that recommendation without qualification.

When you work against these criteria with one common purpose and support each other, in your overlapping roles, without exception, your people will follow your working examples and your agencies will produce more work, that will stick out from the ordinary. 99

Most creative directors working for multinationals will admit that these words make sense.

I am here to tell you that they also make money.

For everybody.

XXV

A bond of trust.

"Are you sure ole Hank done it this a-way"

- from a song by Waylon Jennings

BY definition, the evaluation of a creative approach has to be subjective.

We win with 'one-to-one' crafted advertising, when we hit the buttons of a lot of 'subjectivities' in a single go.

We craft pieces of commercial communication that have to work: Every single hit. Every time. No composer, no poet, no author, no playwright ever had to perform under this *daily* commercial imperative.

In the past few chapters, I have tried to share with you one such subjectivity: An individual point of view.

But all of this wisdom, all of this knowledge, is not worth a hill of beans without the trust and faith of clients who, after all, bet on our skill and ideas with real money.

I might sound old-fashioned, but I think handling someone's money is a sacred trust that carries with it, in every case, its own imperatives. It demands that we give the job at hand our everything. That we keep all expenses up front and pre-determined. That we recommend what is best for the advertiser — spend a dollar where just a dollar will suffice. Not ten, where five will do.

A business that lives on the commission system has to not only be fair, but be seen to be fair to its clients.

Ultimately, of course, this series of chapters has been dedicated to you, the client.

You are the real star of the show. Without your money and your confidence — without your trust — we could never stand and try to rise to the heights that are possible. And we couldn't try as often as we do, to raise the bar after every jump.

I think one of the best examples of this trust and confidence — this bond — that led to extraordinary advertising, was the deal that Pete Townsend, innovative Avis Rent-a-Car chief executive, made with Bill Bernbach of Dolye Dane Bernbach in New York over twenty years ago.

This was a partnership that led to an entire company being advertised as *less* than the best.

And changed rent-a-car advertising as a result. And it introduced something called credibility into our business, once and for all. And raised Avis sales by up to 35%.

"Avis. We're Number Two, so we try harder."

Peter and Bill shook hands on a pact that was typed and framed by the client and hung in DDB as well as the offices of Avis key employees before a word of advertising was created.

Here is what the memo said:

AVIS RENT-A-CAR ADVERTISING PHILOSOPHY

1. Avis will never know as much about advertising as DDB, and DDB will never know as much about the rent-a-car business as Avis.

2. The purpose of the advertising is to persuade the frequent business renter (whether on a business trip, a vacation trip, or renting an extra car at home) to try Avis.

3. A serious attempt will be made to create advertising with five times the effectiveness (see 2 above) of the competition's advertising.

4. To this end, Avis will approve or disapprove, not try to improve, ads which are submitted. Any changes suggested by Avis must be grounded on a material operating defect (a wrong uniform, for example).

5. To this end, DDB will only submit for approval those ads which they as an agency recommend. They will not "see what Avis thinks of that one".

6. Media selection should be the primary responsibility of DDB. However, DDB is expected to take the initiative to get guidance from Avis in weighting of markets or special situations, particularly in those areas where cold numbers do not indicate the real picture. Media judgments are open to discussion. The conviction should prevail. Compromises should be avoided.

I am happy to also dedicate this series on "Understanding Advertising" to this bond of trust between advertising and agency.

For this is the bond that creates the best advertising in the world.

XXVI

The sound of one hand clapping.

"Being on the tightrope is living; everything else is just waiting."

- *Karl Wallenda*

"**W**E are sorry, but the editor's indecision is final."

- Bill Mellor, Asian correspondent for Sydney Sun-Herald, talking about his last editor (in the FCCT house magazine).

Mr. Mellor, like many of us in the communications game, must have come across an executive who had to serve more than one master. The pressures of business can sometimes conflict with the main aim of just putting out a great paper.

Or writing the ultimate, dramatic, different, persuasive and — heck, immortal—ad!

Because the more different it is, the more difficult it is for us to sell it to you, the client. And if the difference comes down to keeping your account in our agency, or losing your business, what do you think we are going to say?

Not too many years ago, the Sultan of one of those Trucial States around the Gulf of Oman admitted to stashing a lot of his new-found wealth around the palace under various mattresses. A visiting dignitary who had the potentate's trust and confidence commented on this phenomenon and suggested that the Sultan hire an Englishman as consultant, like some of the neighbouring states. "An Englishman!" said the Sultan. "Okay. But if you're going to find me an Englishman, please make sure that it is an Englishman with one hand!"

This confused the visitor: "But why an Englishman with only one hand, Excellency?"

"Because then," said the Sultan, "he won't carry on like the other English consultants I have hired in the past. Every time I disagree with their recommendation or proposal, they always say: 'But on the *other* hand ...'"

While I hasten to reassure my English friends that this joke is not aimed at them (they have simply ruled so much of the world for so long that some of these anecdotes do end up pointing in their direction!), the fact is that we advertising people have become better known more for our, er, flexibility in these situations than most other folk. And that's not so good.

All the Sultan wanted, like any good client, was decent advice, in return for the gold he put on the table. And a little bit more. He wanted people with courage of their convictions. He expected the consultant to stand by his recommendations. But if the threat is having your head cut off or being put in some desert dungeon for the rest of your life, I don't blame those consultants of yesteryear for staying nimble-footed in foreign climes.

In our business, some of us consider losing an account almost as bad a fate

Let's Get Rid of Management

People
don't want
to be
managed.
They want
to be led.
Whoever heard
of a world
manager?
World leader,
yes.
Educational leader.
Political leader.
Religious leader.
Scout leader.
Community leader.
Labor leader.
Business leader.
They lead.
They don't manage.
The carrot
always wins
over the stick.
Ask your horse.
You can *lead* your
horse to water,
but you can't
manage him
to drink.
If you want to
manage somebody,
manage yourself.
Do that well
and you'll
be ready to
stop managing.
And start
leading.

A United Technologies ad in The Wall Street Journal that's sort of different. I like that.

(understandable, too, considering how hard it is to land your business in the first place), so any courage from us should be more than just tolerated. It needs nurturing and encouragement.

In a fascinating book called "Leaders: The Strategies for Taking Charge," authors Warren Bennis and Burt Nanus interviewed almost a hundred leaders in business to find out what attitudes and techniques made these people successful. Here is what Franklin Murphy, chairman of the Times-Mirror Publishing Co, had to say:

> **People have to have stake in an idea if they participated in its creation; they'll work much harder, in a much more dedicated way to bring it to success.**

Your consultants, on any side of the marketing fence, are on the same side as you. If they are not, heart and soul, *make* them a part of your team. Or you won't be getting your dollar's worth.

William Kieschnick, president of ARCO, put it this way in the same book:

> **Early in my career, I was working for several leaders in this company who were important role models ... they took risks on exploratory wells and since it was an uncertain situation, they tolerated dissent and other ideas from one another before they hammered out a course of action ... Ideas were important and creative tension was accepted as a working tool, and these things meant a lot in shaping my young life and my values.**

I don't think anybody ever lost too much money by simply listening to somebody else (as opposed to acting on bad advice: but then, if you think you are getting bad advice, change your advisers). And if you are applying for good advice in an area outside your field, stop second-guessing and quarterbacking from the sidelines.

Conviction — utter, complete, solid conviction — is the greatest fruit that an advertising adviser can bring to your business. He takes your account in one hand and, possibly, his income on the other, when he comes trying to sell you something different and difficult. And if he is still thumping tables after you start shaking your head, applaud him.

Because he is clapping, too, you see.
But it's tougher on him.
He is trying to clap with one hand.

XXVII

Are art directors more important than copywriters?

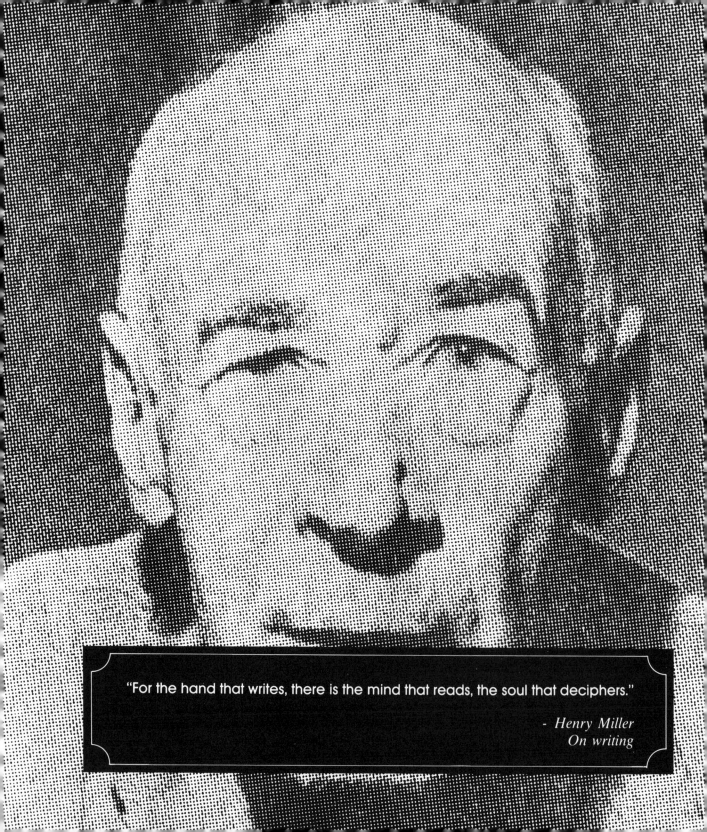

"For the hand that writes, there is the mind that reads, the soul that deciphers."

- Henry Miller
On writing

T's like one of those old trick questions that a biased journalist would ask of old Tammany Hall politics: "Excuse me, congressman, is it true that you've stopped beating your wife when you get drunk these days?"

It is difficult to answer without implicating yourself in some way. And to ask (as, surprisingly, many many people still do) which is more important in the art director/copywriter duo, is to admit that one of them is more important.

And that is simply not true.

But before I explain, let me tell you what I did before I wrote this chapter. I asked some of my friends to answer the same question, promising the wittiest reply a bottle of champagne. The reply I got from John Turnbull, senior writer at Saatchi & Saatchi, London, easily won the bubbly. (Come on down, John, the Dom's on ice!):

Sixteen Self-Explanatory Answers:

1. Q: *What is an art director?*

A: Someone who lacks the skill to be a finished artist and the personality to be an account man.

2. Q: *How did the copywriter get crushed to death?*

A: He got in front of his art director on the way up to the stage to pick up an award.

3. *If art directors are so bloody visual, how come they have to set everything 25 times 'just to see what it looks like, mate'.*

4. Q: *Why did the art director cross the road?*

A: Why do art directors do anything?

5. Q: *Why did the Singapore art director cross the road?*

A: Because he saw Neil French do it.

6. *Being an art director is the most one can say for unskilled labor.*

7. *Art directors say that after a few years, all those girls at casting sessions are "just meat".*

Maybe... but have you ever met one who's a vegetarian?

8. Q: *What's the difference between an elephant and an art director?*

A: Well, an elephant has a huge head and a tiny brain and an art director... God, what *is* the difference between an elephant and an art director?

9. *"Doctor, Doctor... I keep thinking I'm an art director."*

"Go and work at O & M (or Lintas, or JWT, or any agency name!)... you'll meet six people with the same problem."

10. Here's a trick question.

Q: *Who's the art director on Ford who drives a Mercedes?*

A: I warned you it was a trick question: if you've seen the ads, you know there is *no* art director working on the Ford account.

11. They say copywriters are failed authors, art directors are failed artists and account men are failed human beings.

That's not quite true.

Most art directors are just failed art directors.

12. Q: *What is an art director?*

A: A primitive device for turning trees in to waste paper.

13. Q: *How do you get eight art directors into a Volkswagen Beetle?*

A: Tell them it's a vintage Porsche.

14. *When God made art directors... he laughed.*

15. *It's quite untrue that art directors buy Range Rovers because they can't spell Porsche.*

Have you ever seen an art director tying to spell "Range Rover..."? R-A-I...

16. *I hate art directors because they can say things in very few words.*

That's because they only know a "very few words".

Naturally, the above does not reflect my views (or John's for that matter: he has worked with some of the best art directors in the world including my last art director, Bruce Baldwin, who will put a contract on John Turnbull when he reads this!), but it does show that art directors are a much misunderstood race.

I am a writer. I write campaigns every week. But I know this: writers do get away with murder. We stand in the glory of applause, suave and articulate, while the poor art chap who made us look good in the first place is often shoved to the sidelines. This is a hangover from the days when print media was king, and creative directors were actually called copy chiefs (now we have titles like "World Creative Director" which was, before all this, an honorific reserved for the Almighty). In the old days a copy person would write the headlines and the copy, go to all the client meetings and slip final approved copy under the door of the art guy who would be told what to do with the visual.

Giants of the industry in America, like Bill Bernbach, changed all that many years ago.

They proved that the consumer does not look for either art or copy in an ad. The consumer is affected by (or not affected by!) the IDEA behind the ad. Over the last 25 years in the free world, more and more agencies came to see that since the IDEA was the main task, the main opportunity, it made more sense to field a team of two people towards solving it. It turned copy people and art people into advertising people. It virtually doubled the brainpower that was now available to a client on every piece of commercial communication.

One of the first decisions I made when taking over the creative function of the largest advertising agency in this region last year was to pair all the senior creative group heads into two-person teams at the head of each group: one art, one copy. This not only made them into working teams (as well as having a supervisory function) and sent the right message to the over 50 writers, art directors and visualisers in the agency, it also immediately improved the quality of advertising produced in the agency. Instead of rewarding writers over art directors, we reward *idea-generators,* and a professionally motivated *team* can generate an idea much better than one person.

A writer-art director team should work together on an idea right from the start. They should not be thinking art or copy when they first sit down (or stand and yell!) together. They should spend by far the majority of their time thinking about the advertising solution. The actual writing or art direction is simply craft that should be employed in the end to make the winning idea work best in the final communication.

As I have often said in these pages, an ad, to be worth a damn, has to be different and daring and relevant and dramatic and persuasive and involving. So the team we are talking about has to create a small miracle every day.

Perhaps even a major miracle.

Under this sort of stress, would you begrudge an adman a little help? Let me leave you with a little thought from Christopher Logue, who once described the process of creativity in this way:

Come to the edge.
We might fall.
Come to the edge.
It's too high!
COME TO THE EDGE!
And they came
and he pushed
and they flew.

XXVIII

Are you tired of your advertising campaign?

"Corporations, I am afraid, are persons, born like the rest of us imperfect and subject to sin."

- *Paul Samuelson, Nobel Prize-winning economist.*

**AVE you read," once demanded an old girl friend, *"Play it Like it Lays* by Joan Didion?"

"Unh-huh," I said, partly because I hadn't and partly because my mouth was full of cornflakes at the time.

"It is so depressing, it makes you want to slit your throat," she said.

"Unh-huh," I said, having more important things to think about than Joan Didion, for goodness sake. But then she said something that made me sit up and notice.

"I've read it about eighteen times."

Obviously, she is my ex-girl friend now (I mean, *Joan Didion!* What can I tell you?) but she inadvertently made an interesting point; people will go on trying to repeat an experience if it touches them in some way, long after it has appeared to have lost its surprise and freshness.

There are still many people around who dress and cut their hair according to film stars that went out with black and white. There are still people around who try to look like James Dean or Marlon Brando. In Sydney, while working on a weekend radio show, I once met someone who had seen The Rocky Horror Show forty-one times!

Avis Rent-a-Car came out with the *"We're Number Two so we try harder"* campaign over two decades ago, but they still use it around the world. They dropped the "Number Two" part in many markets as they got successful.

Success, in fact, seems to go hand in hand with consistency. Wisk managed to own *"Ring around the collar"* and Colgate still mines gold with *"Ring of Confidence"* in many markets, after all these years. After 10 years of *"reaches the parts other beers cannot reach"*, Heineken continues to bring a witty, refreshing new meaning to the line, constantly making it work harder than the year before. Closer to home. Singapore Girl has made what could have been just another airline *"a great way to fly"* for almost 15 years. Rather than chopping and changing with each new management team, these are just a few of the many advertising successes that have built each year on the money they spent the year before.

Reproduced on the next page is an ad that you might recognize, except that it was created in 1954! That's right. The Marlboro Man is about 34 years old, as is the campaign for the largest selling cigarette brand in the world.

It was created when Mr. Leo Burnett still had a lot to do with his agency in Chicago, with Draper Daniels and Bill Young and Jack O'Kieffe. And when these boys took on this project for Philip Morris Inc, Marlboro was a little known upscale brand mostly

181

The 1954 Marlboro ad that never grew old. And what with Philip Morris now making multi-billion dollar bids, this cowboy must have had something to do with the company's success.

bought by women and pseudosophisticates.

Imagine that. A Marlboro for women?

But that's not all. Here are some of the other factors the agency had to deal with before creating the advertising:

1. The temptation to, somehow, keep their old consumer base even though they suddenly had to appeal to a mainstream, broad audience, but now with a more popular priced brand.

2. Communicate that they had a new, more flavorful tobacco blend, a new filter and an exclusive new type of crush-proof, flip-top pack.

3. The temptation, more than anything else, to focus on the new package because it was, quite simply, the most significant advance in cigarette packaging since the introduction of the soft pack almost 38 years before the launch!

4. And to meet the client's objective that said: *"Marlboro is a cigarette designed for men, that women dislike".* (Source: Julian Watkins: *100 Greatest Advertisements.*)

To my mind there are many factors that contribute to the success of this incredibly simple ad.

But RESTRAINT would surely have to be a major factor. To resist highlighting the greatest packaging innovation for 38 years for a higher aim (long term benefit instead of quick "conversation piece" sales) shows a degree of guts.

In fact, intestinal fortitude figures prominently when one researches the Marlboro story. The early copy testing for the concept was (and I believe would still be, given available techniques) negative. Yet, they went ahead.

With this kind of relaunch, it takes some serious decision-making to get a project like this off the ground. When they chose the cowboy, for instance, they had the sense and the gumption to add the tattoo on his hand to differentiate the Marlboro Cowboy from the other he-men that the competition was given to using. This, too, would have taken someone in authority who was willing to take a chance.

So, what is it that makes the client change campaigns?

The answer is: clients simply get tired of their campaign. I mean, you've probably seen it a billion times before it goes on air. You were involved with the concept. It was presented to you on storyboard. You sat through the changes. You researched the animatic, very often to the point where the original idea has been diffused. And when it was on air, you probably saw it every night for a week. So did your account director. And it's all over bar the shouting. Yawn. Good night.

Everybody and their family, in effect, have by now seen the campaign. *Except the consumer!*

Very often, client management teams find it easier to take the decision to change the advertising because it is an easier decision to make rather than fixing the distribution or the pricing or the sales incentives or whatever. Sometimes, campaigns are changed because it is the end of the fiscal year and "isn't it time we took a fresh look at the advertising, er what, Higgins?" For situations such as these, I have a simple rule of thumb that almost always works; *just when the client is beginning to get bored with the campaign, the consumer is just beginning to notice it.*

Unfortunately, some clients buy 'a' press ad or 'a' TV commercial instead of a campaign, and with that kind of myopic thinking, it is much easier to justify fiddling with what are, after all, the components of the campaign.

In my opinion, for what it's worth, changing any part of a campaign is a very serious step.

Almost as serious as changing agencies.

XXIX

Promotions: Read this chapter, win a Rolls!

PLEASE SEND ME A COPY OF THIS
BOOK THAT HASN'T BEEN
DAMAGED BY IMPULSIVE
COUPON CLIPPERS.

NAME_____

ADDRESS_____

_____ ZIP_____

"If you can dream it, you can do it."

- *Walt Disney*

OR, if a Rolls-Royce doesn't grab you, how about a trip for two to the moon and a lifetime supply of Blogg Extra Soft Toilet Paper?

Yes. As you might have guessed, this chapter is about consumer promotions and no, the offers made in this chapter's headline are not legally binding because they only apply to seven-foot-tall Hottentots living in Alaska who respond to me in person before 12 noon today.

But first, let us clarify what we mean by the term "consumer promotions": A consumer promotion is a short-term incentive to the consumer that generally requires a specific action.

So you see, this does not always mean a mandatory purchase of the product. It could mean your mailing in something to receive something. Or a visit to the store to check something on display.

For a very long time, I used to feel terribly confused when someone said "consumer promotions" and I often equated this area with buy-three-get-one-free offers, percentage-off discounts, hidden giveaways and that sort of thing. No wonder I hated them. I felt the area of consumer promotions was something invented by cash-flow driven sales-blip-hungry managers who cared nothing for the future image of the brand that we at "the real agency" worked so hard to build with clever and persuasive ads. These people, I felt, were winning battles of the sales chart but losing the long-term "unique image" war. But the inflation crunch of the Seventies brought in an era where promotions really took off in America.

It become quite acceptable to go into the store with a whole bunch of coupons. Coupon newsletters proliferated and there was one remarkable case of a woman who walked into a store with a wad of coupons and three dollars. She was able to walk out with $150 worth of groceries. In a market where the population had stabilized, and fewer new stores were opening, the fight started to get down to shelf space, pure and simple. This was because, in the aisles where the real blood was being shed, the shelf space your brand wanted had to come from somebody else's shelf space. And since innovation is the life-blood of any packaged brand product reformulations, line extensions, generics and "me-too" chapter alternatives started to spill over into each other. (Visit a store, look at a product category and close your eyes and try to remember what it was like five years ago. You'll find that there are many, many times more brands in that category than there were when you first went shopping.)

187

As media costs continued to climb, manufacturers automatically started to look for promotions to give them "instant response" and accountable sales to justify the effort in trying times.

Somewhere in New York is a self-effacing man called Chuck Mittelstadt who runs the Centre for Advertising Services which is, a trifle too modestly, called "the information facility of the Interpublic Group of Companies". Actually, it is probably, for marketing specific data, information and analysis, the best fund of such knowledge on the planet. Not surprisingly, it is located on the same floor as that of Interpublic Chairman Phil Geier whom I visited when I was over there. While at CAS, I was very impressed by the material made available to me. One of the videos made and distributed by this "facility" is an interview between Mr. Mittelstadt and Len Daykin, a consumer promotions guru, and I owe to them a lot of the material included in this piece. When looking at the figures for 1980, for instance, they found that, in packaged goods alone, the mainstream or image advertising expenditure had been $31 billion. However, in the same year, consumer promotions expenditure had become $47 billion.

In other words, of the total packaged goods expenditure including image advertising and promotions, the latter had formed 61% to the total! And what was more significant, it was accelerating faster (10% a year for promotions versus 8% for 'image' advertising).

For me, that was a turning point. I started to take consumer promotions much more seriously. And while there is limited space here to go into the details of this CAS video presentation, let me share with you some main points:

1. Consumer promotions that do not synergize with the existing image of the brand are only going to give you a short term benefit. In the long term, the "unrelated" promotion will fight against the brand's image. In other words, if you are selling something that has an image for, say, being kind to old ladies, with a money-off deal, ultimately your image will become that of a price cutter, and people will forget what you were known for in the first place. And that's disaster. Because image is the real equity of your brand. Without it, you are just another name in the crowd.

2. Consumer promotions can build both sales and brand image. A promotion for a product that is ideal for old people could do better to offer, for example, a hundred free memberships to a bowling club than a racing car and wild weekend in Vegas. (Though these days, you can't be sure. Maybe, Vegas will pull 'em in faster!)

3. Aggressive image advertising with supportive promotions can both maintain and build sales, but the accent should be on added value. The price should be kept at the original premium, but the consumer can expect, and reasonably receive, something extra. A good example was Nestle's Quik, in a joint promotion with a Nabisco cookie brand that allowed the consumer to get free milk by using the coupons! This way, without cheapening either brand, *added value* was offered, and everybody came out ahead.

In the area of problems of promotion management, there were four specific minefields worth watching for:

1. Inept planning and execution. This was found to be true in both agencies and on the manufacturers' side. But it is interesting to note that the large agencies have, since then, taken gigantic steps to fix this problem by opening specialized companies or departments to plan and execute promotions. One of the leaders in this area, currently would have to be O&M, who seem to have a lead in advertising-related business, along with Saatchis, in some parts of the world.

2. Lack of top-level attention. In mainstream advertising (I know many specialists in related services who hate the term "mainstream", but that's life!), we often get to meet the senior-most members of the client's management team. Promotions people still seem to end up with junior-level executives even though, in some cases, promotions actually involve more expenditure!

3. Need for better training. Len Daykin pointed out that there are very few tools available to promotion people (you can count them with fingers on one hand: like trial promotions, rewarding the current consumer, pre-emptive promotion, etc) and yet the level of training in this burgeoning field is abysmal. People, he said, were still trying to shoehorn unrelated concepts into the promotion rather than starting with strategy and working up from there.

4. Poor record-keeping, also, was an area worth looking into. While ad practitioners could instantly get hold of "indicative" results like day-after recall and so forth, hard data on promotion results were almost never shared with the agency and guarded like some Secret Elixir. Obviously, sharing this knowledge could benefit everyone in getting better results the next time around.

XXX

Corporate advertising: A nice warm feeling.

"When so much attention is paid to the vast power of multinational companies, it is perhaps wise to think of the numbers of international names that have disappeared from the scene, even during our lifetime."

- John Harvey - Jones
Reflections on Leadership

"OF course, I love you."
"The check is in the mail."
"I'm from Head Office and I'm here to help you."

Three examples from "The Four Greatest Lies in the World" (the Fourth Lie,, unfortunately, is unprintable).

Watching CNN Prime News from the U.S. last week, I saw a series of ads for General Dynamics Co. that were basically images meant to illustrate a voice-over at the end of the commercial. The voice turned out to be a quote from someone highfalutin' like John F. Kennedy or Lyndon B. Johnson. Right at the end of this sort of "video quote," the logo of the advertiser appeared with the line: "A strong company for a strong country."

Even though CNN caters to an audience above the national socio-economic average (it is a 24-hour news service, a channel totally devoted to news and views about news), to my mind a corporate ad like that presupposes that everybody watching its message on a mass medium like television is going to know what this company does, because *nowhere in the commercial do you ever find out!*

For a company called General Dynamics, even with a captive market like the Pentagon, a bit more dynamism in the communication wouldn't have come amiss either. Unfortunately, most corporate advertising is usually, uninformative and uninteresting. Because corporate advertising is usually approved by big boards of corporations that can't agree on anything that smacks of anything specific, the communication is usually "blanded out" till it sounds more like a sleepy Sunday sermon than something that ought to go out and compete with the real commercial world. On print. Or on the airwaves.

Which brings to mind the old story of the multinational president who was about to take advantage of the openings in business behind the Iron Curtain. On a train ride with his management team, his Russian guest took out a bottle of vodka, knocked back a couple of swigs and chucked the bottle out of the window. Puzzled, our entrepreneurial businessman is supposed to have asked why, and the Russian replied: "Oh, it doesn't matter, we have lots more vodka where we come from." At this point the Cuban lit up a massive Havana, took a few drags and chucked his cigar out the window. Again, the puzzled president asked why, and the Cuban said: "Doesn't matter. We have plenty of those where we come from." Not to be outdone, the multinational president went over to one of his own company directors and threw *him* out of the window, saying to his

193

Reagan

These ads have nothing, and everything, to do with corporate advertising. A mainstream, action-oriented ad for an insurance company, it reinforces the fact that an ad does not have to be labelled "corporate" to do the job. Every ad should carry the corporate banner and consistently reinforce the corporate as well as the brand or service message. These appeared in a series that had one ad with an electric chair and an armchair (headline: "The one on the right has claimed more lives") and another one with a disturbing quiz with the line: "Answer these questions and work out the date of your own death." Clear, impactful, no-nonsense advertising from a company that quickly carved out its own niche in the public mind.

unnerved audience: "Oh, it doesn't matter, we have plenty of those where we come from....."

Well, in some of my more frustrated moments, I like to think that board director they threw out of the window was the director of corporate planning, because those are usually the chaps who launch worldwide corporate campaigns that are, as the Bard of Avon said probably after he saw one in this series: "full of sound and fury, signifying nothing." Except that these ads don't have too much sound and very little fury.

And for those of my readers who say that my sense of humor is a trifle too scatological sometimes, the following definition is going to irritate you further: "Most corporate advertising," someone once said, "is like kids who relieve themselves in the swimming pool. It's a nice warm feeling, but *no one knows they did it.*" And what, pray tell, is the point of running advertising that no one notices, no one remembers, no one connects with your company and its hopes and ambitions.

Properly done, corporate advertising — or, if you like, projecting a positive and relevant and honest image about your company — can be of inestimable value to you as it touches your staff, your board, your customers and your prospective customers. Your corporate imagery is a short-term as well as long-term investment, and it doesn't start or stop when you run a few full-page ads in the newspaper. Your corporate image doesn't mean just getting your letterheads right, your envelopes on fine paper and a "dynamic" logo with racing stripes or a "hi-tech" typeface to show your company's arrival in the modern age (though, collectively, all these and more can be important, and a unified look can keep your message coherent).

The first thing to work out is who you really are because, obvious though it may seem, corporate imagery should have some contact with reality. If you project one image because that is what you think your customers really want, or where you want to get to, and the people working for you think they are something else, you lose out on two counts: whatever they tell their friends and relatives is going to be different from what you are spending a lot of money saying. At a minimum of, say, six friends and relatives per employee in a company of 2,000 employees, that lost audience works out to 12,000 people. And these are probably considered the most authoritative people that *other* people listen to when they want to find out more about your company. Second, you will have missed out on internal communications: if corporate imagery is also meant to communicate with your own people, to enthuse them and give them a sense of pride and belonging, incredulity can have a negative instead of positive effect.

195

Campaign, which happens to be the leading British magazine for the advertising business, carried a series about corporate communications in its September 30, 1988, issue. In this issue, John Simmons, a corporate identity specialist at Newell & Sorrell, pointed out that though Thatcher and the Conservative Party are consistently disliked (and consistently successful), they are respected because of the very clear sense of identity. And while stressing that corporate identities grow "from the inside outwards," he said: *"Corporate identity is about finding and then expressing the inner drive and personality of a company."*

And how important is this projection of your inner soul? Globe, the largest investment house in the world, said the following in the context of their investment policies: *"We are successful entrepreneurs investing in companies run by successful entrepreneurs. We monitor commercial activities of people and groups of people. Their styles of management become their trademarks. When they appear in corporate situations ideally suited to their style of operation, we are prepared to invest."*

From the same valuable issue of *Campaign,* a quote from Gray Titterton, chief executive of the Osca Communications Group, highlights another core advantage of properly thought-out corporate communications: "Much time, effort and money is spent on brands. The value of strong franchises for brands is incalculable. Often they are badly undervalued and predators slip in through the back door and purchase the entire company at a relatively modest price. Every reason, therefore, to develop not just brand strategy but a *company* strategy that *adds value to the keeper of the brands."*

One of the joys of writing this book has been the fact that, whenever I hunted long enough, I was able to find experts in areas I knew less about to explain things in a pithy and direct manner, much better than I could ever have done. In the process, I learned a lot.

So what better note to end this chapter and this book than yet another quote from John Simmons on corporate communications: *"And finally, trust your own judgment. Don't fall back on customer market research that will invariably favor the comfortable in preference to the challenging. If your identity is about the personality of your company, then you and the people who work with you are best-placed to decide what is right."*

Thank you and good luck.

Acknowledgements and Inspiration.

FIRST, I would have to acknowledge **Al Ries** and **Jack Trout,** the guys who wrote "Positioning: The Battle for Your Mind" and not only taught me so much by doing so, but gave me the idea of writing a series of articles before attempting a book.

From **Linda Ellerbee's** book, "So It Goes" I gained a couple of anecdotes and the remarkable story about **George Bush** which I wrote about. This eventually, with a new Bush and new election results, even got me a letter of thanks from the President!

Peter Rogen, of Peter Rogen and Associates in New York, personally taught me some presentation techniques which I started using effectively immediately. And that is why I plug him so heavily in my book. The Rogen technique works.

In this book, I have included enough salutes to the dead and the immortals of our business. Let me, for a second, remember the living. All of these people taught me more than I knew before I met them: **Frank Lowe, Phil Gier, Jay Chiat, Dave Trott, Ed McCabe, Philip Adams, Martin Boase, Tony Brignull, Roger Neil, Alyque Padamsee, Bruce Baldwin and Bob Mitchell. Bruce Baldwin** also did the cartoons that you saw in this book.

Nigel Oakins, the intrepid boss of The Bangkok Post, deserves a special paragraph as the man who first said: *"We've got the articles - why not a book?"*

John Turnbull, a good friend, and a warm and witty human being, died the week that the first edition of this book went to the printers. Since he is quoted quite heavily in the chapter dealing with art directors and copywriters (chapter XVII) I called up his family and one of his best friends to read the final galleyproof of the chapter to them. To their credit, they said, "Don't change a word." I didn't.

Canna Kendal (UK), **Gillian Davidson** (SE Asia), **Claire Worthington, Michael Baker** (Australia) and **Dale Cunningham** (USA) are what are known in the trade as head-hunters. For all of them, I was a challenge in placement. They tried hard in markets where sometimes people would say "Oh, he's a copywriter? What *language* does he write in?" All of them were not always successful in getting me a job, but they sure tried. You are the unsung heroes and heroines of our business.

Many of us dip into the advertising trade press for the weekly happenings in our industry. Or the annual list of advertisers when we are looking for new business and their list of ad agencies when we want to check our place on the billings ladder. But this is a 'thank you' on behalf of those of us who actually read every page, for all those Special Reports that focus on the different issues and disciplines in our business. I include, in Australia, *B&T Magazine* and *ADNEWS* and *WIP;* in the UK, *Campaign; Media* and *Asian Advertising & Marketing* in S.E. Asia and *Ad Age* and *ADWEEK* in the USA.

For some of the quotes my thanks to 'Sword Point' by **Harold Coyle,** who must have had fun reading all that juicy war material in the first place.

Associated Press supplied some of the photographs from New York to Bangkok pretty quickly. Thanks, guys.

In this salute, the following people also deserve mention, for reasons of my own in no particular order: **Jonathan Coleman, Ctar Sudasna, Julie French, Fred Zimmerman, Peter Handel-Mazetti, Ken Brady, Les Luxford, Hasan Basar, John Dux, Denis D. Gray, Vichai Suphasomboon, Norman Vale** and **Joyce Rainat.**

A special thank you to **Bert Romero,** the man who, as editor of the Business Post, first took the chance and invited me to do the series that led to this book. Khun **Nartnittha Jirarayapong** did a great job at the paper to keep this book project alive and Khun **Kanit Nontapaoraya,** now with Far East Advertising in Thailand, did a remarkable job with the design and typography.

This chapter of acknowledgements would be incomplete without a word to all those talented people I have worked with — to create ads that won us applause and money. Both **Bill Bernbach** and **David Ogilvy,** giants of our industry, said that when they started their business, they looked for talented people who were also 'nice' people. This is a luxury I have not always been lucky enough to indulge in every time. Some of the giant talents I worked with also had giant egos — and some of them were, in a word, bastards. As long as someone has talent, I'll put up with their idiosyncrasies. Give me talent over 'nice' anyday. As long as they are *winners,* I don't mind working with them. Learning from them.

So here, I salute the talented. And I also salute the bastards. I learned from both categories. Because such is reality, between the commercial breaks.

Finally, a quick "Hi, Mom". In this case, her name is **Pushpa Marwah,** and I bet she'll tell everyone to buy the book, and to my dad **Nanak Chand Marwah** who will, I hope, finally believe that advertising is a serious business and my brother **Ranjan Marwah** in Hong Kong who'll never let his family feed me another meal unless I mention his group of companies which include outdoor media and head hunting.

Thanks, folks.

HOW TO BUY THIS BOOK

A very simple way would be : send us a check or charge by credit card.

At US $24.95 *per copy* (with US $3 extra per copy for packaging and handling) you're *already* saving money. Millions of dollars can be saved by the wisdom and experience in these pages. All you have to do is send in a check or charge by credit card and we'll send you the number of copies you want when the money has been cleared.

If you are interested in ordering more than fifty copies, you could contact us by telephone, fax, or letter at the address mentioned in the coupon.

This book could start developing business for you, or your associates, immediately.

OPTION ONE

I want .... books immediately at US$24.95 per copy (for packaging & handling add US$3 in the U.S. and Canada and 25% of the total order for foreign).

For quantity discounts, please contact the AMA.

☐ Enclosed is my check.
Charge to: ☐ Visa ☐ MasterCard ☐ American Express

Total (US$) enclosed ....

My name is ....

My address is ....

....

....

Tel. no. ....

OPTION TWO

Please contact me urgently. I am interested in more than fifty copies.

My name is ....

My address is ....

My phone is .... Telex: ....

Fax: ....

American Marketing Association
250 S. Wacker Drive, Suite 200, Chicago,
IL 60606-5819, U.S.A., Tel: (312) 648-0536, Fax:
(312) 993-7540 (Business Director).